albuquerque: spirit of the new west

Starlight Publishing

Rick Homans
Chairman/CEO

Missy Penor
Associate Publisher

Dovya Friedman
Editor

Carla Genoni
Managing Editor

Audrey Troche
Production Manager

Robyn Rissman
Editorial Assistant

Andrea Hart
Associate Art Director

Daphne Dobecki
Production Director

Jake Pacheco
Production Artist (sponsors)

Heather Scanlon
Production Artist (sponsors)

Jane Burak
Controller/CFO

Tamera Sparks
Office Manager

Wardie Hennessy
Credit Analyst

Steven Roberts
Director of Distribution

Sheila Carter
Sales Assistant

Donna Busby
Account Executive

Temple Kelleher
Account Executive

Vaughn Wedeen
Creative

Rick Vaughn
Principal & Senior
Creative Director

Foster Hurley
Creative Director

Chip Wyly
Production Artist

Karen Raff
Project Coordinator

Flying Color Graphics

Prepress 800.544.0518

Published in conjunction
with the Greater
Albuquerque Chamber
of Commerce.

contents

from the publisher

Here in Albuquerque, we are accustomed to living without boundaries. There are big skies, brilliant sunsets, cultural journeys and endless opportunities. Presenting this expanse within the distinct confines of front-and-back book covers is an enormous challenge. It is also an education. As we put these pages together we found ourselves grateful for the shopping malls, highways, industries and technology that make us a modern American community. Increasingly, however, we focused on the things that make Albuquerque different from all other cities: Indian pueblos, green chile, hiking trails, open space, cultural festivals, Spanish art, hot-air balloons, Route 66, and so much more. Our differences and diversity are what make Albuquerque special. Albuquerque: Spirit of the New West is a celebration of everything that makes our city unique—a look at the past and at what we are today, and a glimpse of what we will become. We hope you enjoy.

As with any work of this magnitude, there are many people to thank. Some of them, such as Albuquerque Mayor Jim Baca and Bernalillo County Commission Chairman Tom Rutherford, supported the project from the beginning. The Greater Albuquerque Chamber of Commerce also lent its support to the book from its inception, and we thank its president, Terri Cole. The driving creative forces behind this publication were Dovya Friedman, its editor, and Rick Vaughn, its creative director. Without their unfailing energy and commitment, this book would not have been possible. I thank the many sponsors of this project, who provided us the opportunity to work with some of the best photographers and writers in Albuquerque. And, finally, a heartfelt thank you to the entire staff of Starlight Publishing for going beyond the call of duty to produce a book of unparalleled quality.

Rick Homans, Publisher

March, 2000

contributors

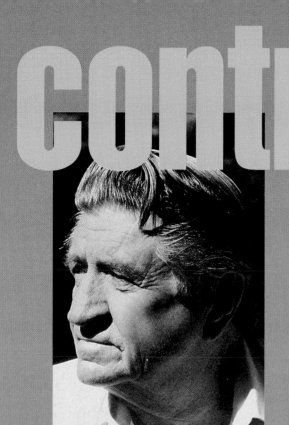

Max Evans, writer, *Love of a City*

Max Evans, born in Ropes, Texas, has lived and worked in New Mexico since age 11, when he first went to work on a cow ranch south of Santa Fe. Since then, he has enjoyed many careers: soldier, rancher, miner, professional artist, and writer. He has also been involved extensively in the film industry, both in New Mexico and in Hollywood. Mr. Evans has published such well-known works as *The Rounders*, *The Hi Lo Country* (both of which have been made into feature films) and *Bluefeather Fellini in the Sacred Realm*. Besides his books, Mr. Evans' writing has appeared in regional and national journals and magazines, and has won many awards and honors. Max Evans and his wife Pat have called Albuquerque home since 1968.

"This city has greatly gifted my family for thirty-three years, allowing us to follow our chosen creative work. When we moved here it was a big, small-town. Now it is a city with some leftover small-town in it. With candor, and some courage, I predict that within the next quarter century it will, it must, become a culture icon to the world. The recipe is all here. Saludos amigos."

1
1

Rick Vaughn, designer, *Albuquerque: Spirit of the New West*

Mr. Vaughn was born in Dallas, Texas and moved to Albuquerque in 1980. He is a principal and senior creative director of Vaughn Wedeen Creative, Inc. The design firm's capabilities include corporate identity, signage, exhibits and environmental design, as well as web site design. Vaughn Wedeen's work has been recognized in a number of national and international trade publications and events including *Graphis*, *Communications Arts*, *Print*, New Mexico Advertising Federation, and New York Art Directors Show. Mr. Vaughn's projects range from packaging and interiors to furniture, trade show display, site signage and lighting design, as well as ergonomic design of office environments.

"Working on this book was special because this is the place I picked to live. Like many people, something drew me to Albuquerque. The project reintroduced me to those feelings and made me feel good about the city."

Michael Barley

Michael Barley has been a commercial photographer in Albuquerque for over 13 years, during which time he has worked with every major advertising and design firm in the city. He has also worked with the city's banks, hospitals, major health-care providers and educational institutions. His work has earned numerous awards in local, regional and national competitions.

Miguel Gandert

Miguel Gandert, a native of Española, New Mexico, is a documentary and fine arts photographer. He is an associate professor at the Department of Communication and Journalism at the University of New Mexico. Mr. Gandert's photographs have been shown in galleries and museums throughout the world and are in numerous public collections.

Eric O'Connell

Eric O'Connell is a commercial freelance photographer. A native of New Mexico, he has been based here since 1982. His clients include *Time*, *People*, *Newsweek*, *Fortune*, and *Forbes*. When not shooting you can find him on a bicycle in Albuquerque or learning to surf in San Francisco.

Darren Poore

Darren Poore works as a commercial photographer in Albuquerque. Between spending time with his daughter, riding his mountain bike, and eating green chile stew, Poore finds time to shoot editorial photography for local and national publications. His images have appeared in such magazines as *Photo District News*, *Maximum PC*, *Bicycling*, and *USA Weekend*.

Jerry Rabinowitz

Jerry Rabinowitz is an award-winning commercial and architectural photographer, and his work is featured in regional and national publications as well as several books about the Southwest. Mr. Rabinowitz was co-president of the New Mexico chapter of the American Society of Media Photographers (ASMP).

writers

Robert Reck
Robert Reck is a New Mexico-based architectural and interior design photographer whose assignments have taken him around the world. He holds a Master's degree in Fine Art photography from the University of New Mexico. A contributing photographer to *Architectural Digest*, he has also been published in *Architecture*, *Architecture Record*, and *Interior Design*.

William Stone
William Stone is an Albuquerque-based photographer specializing in the landscapes and ancient archaeological sites of the American Southwest. His images have been published in a variety of books, magazines, calendars, and other publications in the genre. Mr. Stone's work has been exhibited in several museum, gallery, and permanent installation venues.

Wendy Walsh
Wendy Walsh began her career in the alternative press, where she focused on in-depth photo essays on various social issues. Her work has appeared in such publications as *The New York Times*, *Doubletake*, *Sports Illustrated*, *Forbes*, *Ms.*, *Glamour*, *Columbia Journalism Review*, and *New Mexico* magazine.

ADDITIONAL PHOTOGRAPHY:

Mo Palmer
Albuquerque Museum
Mo Palmer is Archivist at the Albuquerque Museum, where she manages historic photographs, conducts the oral history program, curates exhibits, and produces history documentaries. Ms. Palmer is a lifelong New Mexico resident.

Marc Piscotty
Marc Piscotty worked for more than five years as a staff photographer at *The Albuquerque Tribune*, where he won regional and national awards for his photography.

EDITOR:

Dovya Friedman
Albuquerque: Spirit of the New West
Ms. Friedman moved from independent film work in New York to magazine editing for Starlight Publishing in Albuquerque, where she's lived since 1994.

Stephanie Hainsfurther
In the Spirit of Sponsorship — Profiles
Stephanie Hainsfurther is a freelance journalist who has written more than 300 business articles for publications including *New Mexico Business Weekly*, *Business Start-Ups* and *Self Employed Professional*. Her how-to column for entrepreneurs, *Small Business Savvy*, runs in each issue of *New Mexico Woman* magazine.

Foster Hurley
Albuquerque: Spirit of the New West — Text
Foster Hurley is an artist, designer, screenwriter, yoga instructor and cowboy toy collector. He created award-winning print and broadcast campaigns for advertising agencies in New York, Los Angeles, Dallas and Austin before moving to New Mexico in 1995. He has been a creative director at Vaughn Wedeen Creative since 1996.

Sue Vorenberg
In the Spirit of Sponsorship — Profiles
Sue Vorenberg is a national freelance writer and editor based in Albuquerque. She writes regularly about business, technology, science and entertainment for *The Albuquerque Tribune*, the *New Mexico Business Journal*, *Crosswinds Weekly*, and for a series of national environmental science newsletters published by Business Publishers Inc. and CJE Incorporated.

IN THE SPIRIT OF REMINISCENCE:
THE REMEMBRANCE OF THINGS PAST
IS A BITTERSWEET JOURNEY BACK
THROUGH TIME AND PLACE...A
RETRACING OF THE MOMENTS IN A
LIFE SHADED AND TEXTURED BY THE
MILIEU IN WHICH THEY CAME TO PASS.
ALBUQUERQUE STIRS *RECUERDOS*
UNIQUELY ITS OWN...AND AT THEIR
BEST, THEY ARE A LOVE SONG.

LOVE OF A CITY

by Max Evans

I didn't always know about Albuquerque. The first time I ever thought of the Duke City, I was a twelve-year-old boy working on the Rafter EY Ranch on Glorieta Mesa, about 40 miles south of Santa Fe. My boss, Ed Young, and I were riding the rimrock looking for stray cattle. The idea was to scan the ground for tracks, and the tumbled boulders and brush below for the movement of cows, but my eyes were drawn instead to the mysterious mountains in the distance. I imagined them filled with all sorts of streams, ancient ruins, and Indian pueblos.

I asked Ed — at considerable peril; I wasn't being paid twenty dollars a month to study the landscape — "What are those mountains over there?"

With a quick glance he said, "The Jemez. Good wild turkey hunting." Ed was a man of few words.

He did not tell me my vision of Indian pueblos, ruins, and streams was true. In that time of the great and desperate Depression, his thoughts justifiably focused on where the food was located.

My eyes followed the landscape and came to rest on a great array of mountains to the south and west. One loomed larger, more prominent, than the others. I couldn't stop looking at it. Finally, I got up the courage again to ask, "And that one there? What's that one?"

Ed reined up. "That's Sandia. Means 'Watermelon Mountain'."

I was strangely thrilled at the name. From this angle, I could easily imagine the eastern side of the mountain a giant blue watermelon (most of them were bluish-green in those days) sitting in a million-acre garden. It would be years before I learned the name actually came from the unmatchable pink that colors Sandia's western face at day's end.

Ed surprised me by voluntarily adding, "And there's a really big town over there called Albuquerque." The size of the town was relative, of course. He was comparing it to the tiny village of Lamy, New Mexico, where he and his family and his cowboys did their once-a-month shopping and playing.

Little did I know then that someday I would call Albuquerque home, and that there I would fulfill my life's work.

"THAT'S SANDIA.
MEANS 'WATERMELON MOUNTAIN'."

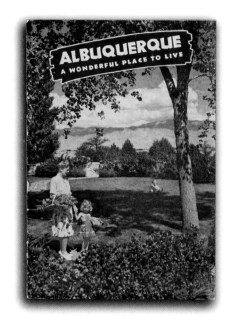

HEADING SOUTH FOR THE WINTERS

It was a simple matter, really, that brought me and my family to Albuquerque.

Being a freelance writer is a tough way to make a living. Fortunately, I had accidentally discovered I could make enough loot from movie options and screenplays to allow me to write what I loved most: novels and short stories. In those days I traveled to Los Angeles on business by train. My wife, Pat, and our twin daughters, Charlotte and Sheryl, would drive me from our home in Taos to the grand Harvey House train station in Albuquerque and put me on the Super Chief, bound for the Land of the Laid Back. When I returned, they would meet me at this famous train station next

to the Alvarado Hotel. We would stay the night in Albuquerque at the Silver Spur, a simple, clean motel whose owners' teenage daughter babysat for us whenever we needed her. We would treat ourselves to Chinese food at what is now New Chinatown,

MOTHER ROAD or maybe steaks at The Paddock Room **ROUTE 66** (sadly, it burned to the ground around 1968). All these establishments were on the famed Mother Road, Route 66.

Our comfortable routine was destined to change. After my family got caught in one too many bad snowstorms between Taos and Santa Fe, I became deeply concerned about their driving me to and from the train station. So, on New Year's Day, 1968, we moved to the city we already cared for — and the round trip to the station went from five hours to fifteen minutes. It was that simple.

LIFE IMITATES ART

If the Great Mystery in the Sky enjoys art — and this must be so — then He or She might well visualize Greater Albuquerque as a framed portrait. The frame's southern side is formed by Kirtland Air Force Base, Sandia National Laboratory, and Isleta Pueblo. Intersecting the picture, the fabled Rio Grande courses twenty-five miles through Bernalillo County, its curving banks embraced by the lush bosque — nature's precious gift of cottonwood groves.

The portrait's western side is framed mainly by the fast-growing town of Rio Rancho. Nearby Petroglyph National Park — containing exceptional rock art of the mystical, ancient Anasazi — contrasts sharply with Rio Rancho's ultra-modern homes and high-tech businesses, most notably microchip giant Intel.

To the northwest lies the village of Corrales, which corners the Duke City with old and new adobe homes and businesses. Its inhabitants love their lush pastures filled with fruit trees, horses, dogs, and sheep with a profound, prideful obsession. Further north is the historical and easy-going town of Bernalillo, which borders Sandia Pueblo. To the northeast lie the village of Placitas and the Sandia foothills, where fine Southwest-style homes have become a part of the landscape.

The portrait of Greater Albuquerque is completed on the east by mighty Sandia Peak. Circling to the east side of this great prominence are several scattered villages of mountain lovers — towns such as Cedar Crest, Edgewood and Tijeras, whose residents would not trade their forested acreages for all of Manhattan Island.

The portrait portrays a landscape as magnificently varied as its people.

(opposite)
(top left)
Petroglyph
National Monume

(top right)
Coronado
National Monume

(lower left)
Isleta Golf Course

(lower right)
Sandia Peak
Ski Area

(this page)
(lower left)
Present day La Posada Hotel lobby
(formerly the downtown Hilton)

(lower right)
The downtown Hilton bar, circa 19

(opposite)
M & J Restaurant and
Sanitary Tortilla Factory

FOOD IS FUN IN OUR CITY AND ON OUR MOUNTAIN

Those who have seen the Grand Canyon, Yosemite Falls, Chaco Canyon, or Paris will never forget them. Yet, like a bear, coyote, cow, or mockingbird, often what we remember best are the places where we've dined and drank with the greatest pleasure. My own personal favorite feed troughs and watering holes during my first decade here were the old downtown Hilton, Al Montes, and El Cid. They all served the finest of foods, and the multicultured ambiance was always special. And they each had one or two owners or managers who gave them a distinct identity — as all successful service businesses have.

Being the pure-bred mongrel that I am, I unabashedly relish the Duke City's multiculturalism. Of course, the uncommon variety of cuisine found here is part of that irresistible charm. I, for one, could enjoyably spend a lifetime here with no other purpose than to seek out and sample the New Mexican restaurants. There are so many of quality, from fancy giants like Garduño's to unpretentious Loyola's Cactus Flower on East Central, to the M & J in the South Valley and El Pinto in the North Valley, where diners enjoy year-round patio dining. Every chile lover to his or her own favored location and taste.

uncommon VARIETY of cuisine

There are almost as many choices of first-class Asian restaurants as there are New Mexican. The search can go on to Greek, East Indian, Italian, French.

Each Albuquerquean, past or present, has his or her own fond Memories of Place. Places such as Neds, the great sports-crowd pleaser; or Paul's Monterey Inn, still solid as the Sandias; or Eddie's Inferno; or the Sunset Inn, where Santa Fe politicos once joined their Duke City colleagues and danced to a big band; or Fred Dunnivan's Mission Inn, where nuclear physicists and Air Force brass mingled with basketball fans, land developers, dice hustlers, and other first-rate outlaws.

(this page)
(top)
Gold Street Caffe

(bottom)
Seasons
Rotisserie & Grill

Early on, my film buddies and I rented a large office space in the old Hilton Hotel. It fronted 2nd Street, at that time right across the street from First National Bank. We worked on a lot of projects for the State Film Commission there and made two documentaries as well. One of them was about Sandia Peak; I called it Every Man's Mountain. The thirty-minute film was narrated by smooth-voiced Rex Allen, who had done narration for more than a hundred Disney films. Sponsored by Datsun, the film was shown locally on Channel 7 (KOAT) and ran for several years on various PBS stations.

I had decided to cover all four seasons on the mountain, so naturally the project took over a year of walking about the great rocky, forested bulk, checking out the wondrous wildlife it nourishes. We became very close that year — the little crew and the mountain, like an old prospector alone in the desert with his burro. Enough time passes and you start to talk with the mountain — or the burro.

EACH ALBUQUERQUEAN, PAST OR PRESENT, HAS HIS OR HER OWN FOND MEMORIES OF PLACE.

After lunchtime on the last day of shooting, I sat down alone on a flat rock at the crest and looked across Albuquerque, marveling at the growing city and the tens of thousands of lives begun and lived out there. I could see all the way to Mount Taylor, over by Grants, and was pleasantly amazed by the vastness of open space still undeveloped. The image of the city viewed from mighty Sandia is indelible. Everyone who cares about people in their place, amidst wide open land, should experience it.

THROUGH A VISITOR'S EYES

Everywhere I have ever traveled or lived, I have heard someone complain, "There's nothing to do in this town." I have never heard a single person voice this complaint in Albuquerque. If it ever does happen, we will just have to forgive them as utterly lacking in imagination or grossly ignorant, and a professional whiner of the first order.

Albuquerque is an addictive city of adventure. Trying to see and absorb all the priceless gifts of our city in a week, a month, or a year would be as difficult as hand digging a ditch both ways at once.

During our more than three decades in Albuquerque, my family and I have hosted countless visitors from all walks of life, due mostly, I suppose, to our own eclectic occupations. Our guests have included the likes of David and Rose Dortort, producer of Bonanza and High Chaparral; Henry (Hank) Fonda, one of the world's great movie stars, who made several films in New Mexico and Albuquerque; top character actors L.Q. Jones, Morgan Woodward, James Gammon, and Slim Pickens; and world-renowned directors Sam Peckinpah (The Wild Bunch), Stephen Frears (Dangerous Liaisons), and Burt Kennedy (Support Your Local Sheriff) — just to touch on a few of the film people who know and love Albuquerque.

We have also hosted famous and infamous writers and painters of every persuasion, geologists, archaeologists, world-champion rodeo hands, numberless

broken-down, working cowboys, worn-out miners and prospectors, struggling farmers, outright-but-entertaining bums and thirty-six-cent con artists of every ilk.

I list these folks to show why it is so very difficult to choose the one visitor who loved our city most of all, who saw it with the sharpest eyes. That person was John Sinor, a San Diego columnist syndicated in over six hundred newspapers worldwide by the Copley Wire Service. John was a handsome man with prematurely gray, wavy hair and the kindest brown eyes I ever saw. In a blurb for a book collection of his columns, I wrote: "The thing that makes Sinor the best is his sense of humanity. He can impale an emotion with six words and create a myriad of visions with six hundred." The man was full of love. That he gave so much of it to Albuquerque was a profound endorsement.

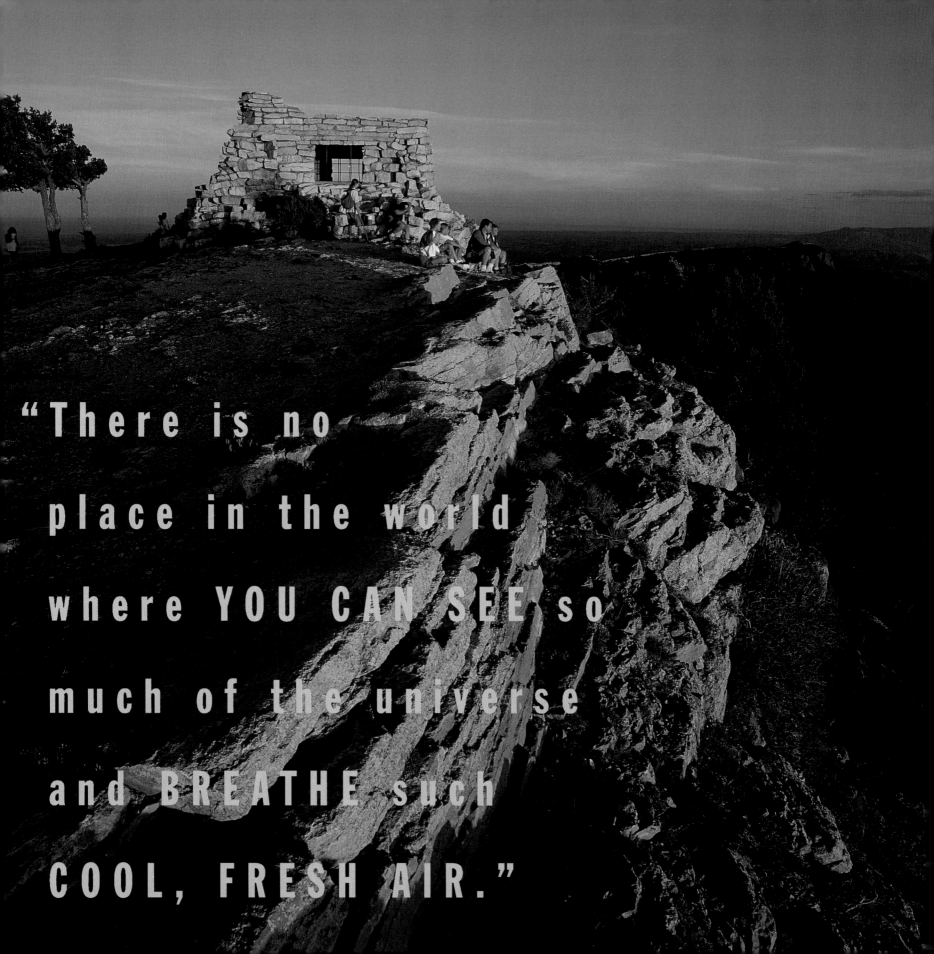

"There is no place in the world where YOU CAN SEE so much of the universe and BREATHE such COOL, FRESH AIR."

When the pressure of John's five-times-a-week deadline mounted to the blowing point, he'd announce to his wife, "I'm ready for my Albuquerque fix." Diane understood and here he would fly.

This world traveler — paid to do so — could hardly wait to get to the top of the Sandia Mountains. It seemed natural, I suppose, since Sandia boasts one of the world's longest tramways — with great dining and viewing at both top and bottom — and unsurpassed views of forested canyons and mighty castles of stone, and treasured glimpses of bear or deer or eagle.

Sometimes I'd drive him around the east side of the mountain; sometimes we'd take the tram. Now, I have an inner-ear problem, so I'd load up on Dramamine so I could exult with him in this experience, enjoying the zillion-mile-view of earth and sky through his wide, wondering eyes. Once, while we were having a sandwich on the wooden deck at the summit, the mountain clouds let loose a few scattered drops of rain — along with a sudden, cracking display of lightning and thunder.

"Isn't this absolutely great?" John beamed.

I was too scared to answer. Finally I stammered, "I'm out of soda," and high-tailed it for what seemed the dubious protection of the diner.

John continued to sit out in the open until the raucous little storm moved on down the crest and dissipated. Only then did I — with cowardly feeling — rejoin him. He had barely noticed my absence, it seemed, because he said, "There is no place in the world where you can see so much of the universe and breathe such cool, fresh air."

He hesitated, looked at me seriously, and continued, "You know, Max, the lightning titillates the air and makes it breathe sweeter."

31

I didn't honestly know, but I wasn't about to dispute a veteran world traveler. And yes, the air was sweet here.

John was an avid shopper. He and I could spend all day meandering through Old Town, enjoying the great jewelry and crafts shops that burst with such abundance and variety that they become celebrations unto themselves. John's oldest son is a priest, and John couldn't wait to bring Father Mike to town to show him the grand old San Felipe de Neri Church on the Old Town Plaza.

Since John lives in San Diego, home to one of the world's largest and most famous zoos, my family and I were surprised at how often he wished to visit ours, the Rio Grande Zoo. I finally became so curious, I asked him why. He answered instantly: "It's friendly and it's not in a hurry."

That statement sums up a lot of the underlying attitude and graciousness of our city's more than three-hundred-year history. We must never let it go.

"IT'S FRIENDLY AND IT'S NOT IN A HURRY."

THE PLACE TO BE — THE CITY TO SEE

It took almost three hundred years from its founding for Albuquerque to reach a population of 300,000. It has taken only thirty more for the metro area to reach nearly 750,000. The majority of Albuquerqueans today should have tons of fun living to see it hit one million residents.

At the close of the twentieth century, Albuquerque has a lot to brag about, especially in the high-tech sector. Sure, Sandia National Laboratory has contributed mightily to almost every phase of the nation's space program, as well as to the fast-as-thought communications of our computerized world. Sure, Bill Gates spawned Microsoft here and went on to become one of the world's richest men. Sure, Intel's huge Rio Rancho plant, which employs thousands, manufactures computer chips that help propel the planet. Sure, the area supports hundreds of other, smaller high-tech companies that strive to be the next Intel...

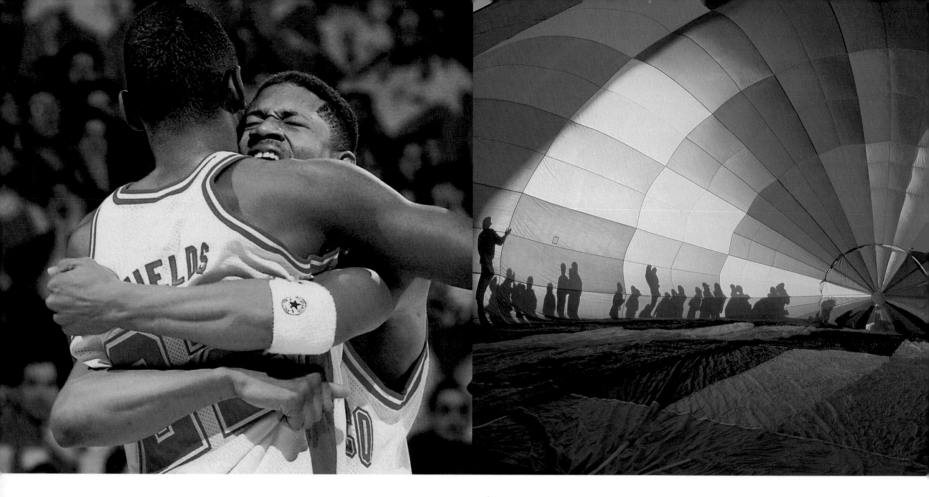

Yet, to my mind, The Pit is the city's Mecca. Yes, our famous basketball

stadium. Because of The Pit and the noble Lobos team, Albuquerque is infiltrated

with hordes of people who, for part of the year, only half-taste their food,

barely notice the natural beauty surrounding them, and neglect their businesses

and jobs to a degree that, elsewhere, would lead to mass firings and bankruptcy.

One of the events that saves these fans from cracking up from seasonal

sports anxiety is the Kodak™ Albuquerque International Balloon Fiesta, the

(opposite)
(left)
Lobo basketball
triumphs at the Pit

(right)
Kodak™
Albuquerque
International
Balloon Fiesta

world's major ballooning festival and most-photographed event. The striking sight of hundreds of rainbow-hued balloons sailing across the vast blue autumn sky is nothing short of magnificent. The annual balloon fiesta draws some one million visitors — in a state with a total population of only two million or so — testament to the magnetic enchantment of this gathering in the sky and on the ground. People come from all over the world for the experience, and the international media let the rest of the world view it vicariously.

The Balloon Fiesta is preceded by one of the nation's top state fairs, featuring Hispanic and Indian villages, horse racing, rodeo, gaming, concerts, midway rides, and arts and crafts exhibits galore. Supreme. Without hesitation, I do declare we have more fine crafts people in our city than the odds would seem to allow. To miss our arts and crafts fairs here is to commit a sin against your personal soul. But there is much you don't want to miss.

Following the Balloon Fiesta, the Indian National Finals Rodeo, held at Tingley Coliseum on the New Mexico State Fairgrounds, features performers and participants from most North American tribes. What a show! And the Gathering of Nations Pow Wow, held each spring at The Pit, is a unique experience.

Speaking again of The Pit, Albuquerque boasts enough artists, writers, and crafts people, to fill that sacred location. One national magazine declared a few years ago that Albuquerque had too many writers. A loud local uproar denied this. Mostly writers, I imagine. No wonder the greatest combat correspondent of World War II, Ernie Pyle, wrote so many letters to his wife stating with heartfelt love how much he wanted to join her at their little home in Albuquerque. He never made it back. Those of us who did give joyful thanks for our good fortune.

Returning to the sports scene, Albuquerque is home to the Unsers, one of the most winning car-racing families in history. Other sports greats with ties to the Duke City include retired or recent world-champion boxers Bobby Foster, Johnny Tapia, and Danny Romero; Tommy McDonald, recently inducted into the NFL Hall of Fame; and Notah Begay, the young Pueblo/Navajo golfer who became the first American Indian to win a PGA Tournament.

Those who participate in, not just watch, sports, will take heart in the fact that the local saying is true: On some winter days, you can literally ski on Sandia Peak in the morning and play golf or tennis later that same day.

No paean to Albuquerque would be complete without mention of the legendary Rio Grande. That bosque-enhanced river has entranced people for centuries. Not only is it a life-giving liquid trail to both body and spirit, but the most written-about river imaginable. There have been more lovers' and liars' tales told about this stream, more stories of six-shooters, cattle drives, and land wars, than can be counted, with even more to come. A lot of them were, and are, true. The river runs through the works of many local writers, and Paul Horgan even won a Pulitzer Prize for his book about it, "Great River: The Rio Grande in North American History." You may have noticed, too, that it shows up in a whole lot of paintings and photographs. For good reason.

Yet despite the peaceful allure of the Rio Grande bosque and the soaring majesty of the Sandias, the soul and the eyes sometimes need the serenity that only vast empty spaces can give. Within one hour of the city limits, in any direction, this can be found. There are spots so wide open and vast, one can gaze restfully into infinity. A precious rarity, indeed, in this overcrowded world.

I have spent the equivalent of several creative lifetimes here since Sandia Peak and the "Big Town" were pointed out to me so many years ago from the lonely, hard-bitten rimrock of Glorieta Mesa. In that time, I have written as many stories, been involved in as many movies, and traveled to as many other cities as strength and time would allow. It has been far more fun than I could handle, full of surprising and exciting escapades, but I sure gave it one helluva go. Thank you mucho, Albuquerque, I love you.

Oh, what a city it was.

Oh, what a city it is.

THERE ARE SPOTS SO WIDE OPEN AND VAST, ONE CAN GAZE RESTFULLY INTO INFINITY."

Sandia Mountains looking west from the wide open spaces of the far West Mesa

In the Spirit of appreciation:

TELLING ONLY ONE STORY IS INSUFFICIENT TO CAPTURE THE TRUE ESSENCE OF A MULTI-FACETED PLACE. THE KNOWING OF A CITY IS THE LEARNING OF MANY STORIES OF MANY PEOPLES...OF VARIED CULTURES...OF RICH TRADITIONS. TO TOUCH ITS *CORAZÓN* IS TO WITNESS A DANCE OF WORDS AND PICTURES.

4
5

Between the *montoñas* and the *mesas* runs a river.

A city that embodies the diversity of cultures

Astride it stands a city.

and breadth of ideals that are uniquely American.

As adventurous Americans began to motor west... some liked it here the very best

o they remained, captured by the beauty of the High Desert. They're still getting their kicks on Route 66.

TO BE
RELOCATED
THROUGH
INDIAN
LANDS

WILL BE FINISHED
READY FOR
PAVING
IN
MARCH 1935

S

66
6

ALBUQ

SUWANEE

66

ALBUQ

LOS LU

26 — ✳ — 14 — ✳ — 33

29

Highway U. S. 66 through Sandia Mountains

The first to settle here were not alone for long.

The middle Rio Grande Valley has embraced the native and newcomer alike.

Sojourners and settlers, proprietors and *patrónes*, farmers and physicists.

Administration Building, Municipal Airport

By planes, trains and automobiles they came.

For their health, for their wealth...

seeking a life of otherness. Knowing

that no matter how the course of history

flowed, life's journey here would

always be *el camino* less traveled.

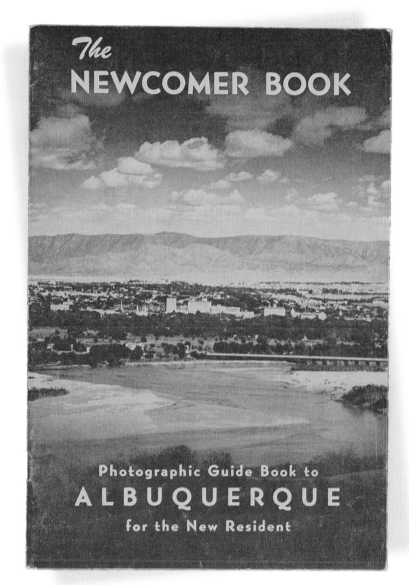

The
NEWCOMER BOOK

Photographic Guide Book to
ALBUQUERQUE
for the New Resident

A L V A

R A D O

H O T E

THE ALVARADO
By Fred Harvey
Albuquerque, N.M.

DINNER SUGGESTIONS

DINING ROOM
Open 12 to 2 p.m. — 6 to 9 p.m.

MAY WE SUGGEST BEFORE DINNER

Manhattan .... .70
Dry Martini .... .65

KING SIZE MARTINI 1.00
(Daily Except Sunday)

HOT WEATHER SUGGESTION

COLD SLICED BREAST OF TURKEY
AND HAM, WALDORF SALAD
ROLL AND BUTTER
COFFEE, MILK, OR ICE TEA
2.00

SALAD PLATES

ALVARADO SALAD BOWL 1.45
CHEF'S SALAD 1.25
SHRIMP SALAD 2.50
SLICED TOMATOES .... .40
HEAD LETTUCE .... .40
PANAMA SALAD, Cottage Cheese 1.25
CHILLED AVOCADO FILLED WITH CHICKEN
SALAD, SLICED EGG, TOMATOES 2.00
(Roquefort Cheese Dressing 10c Extra)

SANDWICHES

BOILED HAM .... .65
MONTE CRISTO 1.50
MANHATTAN 1.50
CLUB 1.25
SLICED CHICKEN .... .95
HAMBURGER, POTATOES .... .75
TOASTED CHEESE AND BACON .... .75
HITCHING POST SANDWICH 1.50

VEGETABLES AND POTATOES

NEW PEAS .... .25
FRESH CARROTS .... .25
GREEN BEANS .... .25
HOME FRIED POTATOES .... .25
FRENCH FRIED POTATOES .... .25
BAKED POTATO .... .30

BEVERAGES

TEA, POT .... .25
COFFEE, CUP .... .15   POT .... .30
SANKA OR POSTUM, POT .... .30
OVALTINE, POT .... .30
BUTTERMILK .... .15
COCOA, POT .... .30
MILK, BOTTLE .... .15

SOUPS AND APPETIZERS

Pot Au Feu Henry IV .... Cup .25, Bowl .35
Chicken Broth With Rice, Cup .25; Bowl .35
Shrimp Cocktail .... .75
Apple Cider .... .25   Tomato Juice .... .20
Fruit Cocktail Supreme .... .65
Jellied Madrilene, Cup .... .25
Half Grapefruit .... .35
Consomme en Tasse, Cup .25
Cold Cream Vichyssoise, Cup .30
Shrimp Cocktail Supreme 1.15
Marinated Herring .... .50
Ripe or Green Olives .... .55
Smoked Salmon .... .60
Mixed Relish .... .50
Celery Hearts .... .50

ENTREES

RED CHINOOK SALMON STEAK SAUTE, RAVIGOTE SAUCE 1.85
FRESH JUMBO GULF SHRIMP SAUTE IN GARLIC OIL, FRA-DIAVOLO 2.50
BROILED COLORADO MOUNTAIN STREAM TROUT, HOTELIERE 2.25
VIRGINIA HAM AND EGGS COUNTRY STYLE, GREEN PEPPER RINGS 1.50
HARVEY HOUSE "SIRLOIN" BUTT STEAK, SAUCE BEARNAISE 2.00
ROAST LOIN OF FRESH PORK, STEWED SANTA ROSA PLUM 1.85
HALF MILK FED CHICKEN, SAUTE UNJOINED, COUNTRY GRAVY 2.10
BREADED VEAL CUTLET, VIENNOISE BUTTERED NOODLES 1.95
FRENCH LAMB CHOPS WITH STUFFED MUSHROOMS, HOTELIERE 2.95

— Choice of Two with the Above —

Cauliflower, Tangy Cheese Sauce   French Cut String Beans, Saute
Baked Potato   Creamy Whipped Potatoes
Chef's Salad in Bowl, Chiffonade
Death Valley Date Salad, Chatelaine Dressing

DESSERTS

PIES: APPLE, APRICOT .... .30
COCOANUT CUSTARD PIE .... .30
BLUEBERRY COBBLER .... .30
FRESH STRAWBERRIES WITH CREAM .... .65
OLD FASHIONED STRAWBERRY
SHORTCAKE, WHIPPED CREAM .... .50
CUP CUSTARD .... .35
VANILLA OR CHOCOLATE CAKE .... .30
WATERMELON .... .45
CANTALOUPE .... .35
FRUIT JELLO .... .30
ICE CREAM, ASSORTED FLAVORS .... .30
SHERBET .... .30
SUNDAE .... .40
FROZEN ECLAIR .... .55

MEXICAN SUGGESTIONS

MEXICAN PLATE: ENCHILADAS, TAMALE, FRIJOLES AND POSOLE 1.35
OUR OWN MADE ENCHILADAS, FRIED EGG HERNANDO 1.25
CHILI CON CARNE .... .50   TAMALES WITH CHILI .... .75

FROM THE BROILER

☆ Starred Items Completed
HARVEY HOUSE SIRLOIN STEAK 4.50
HARVEY JUNIOR SIRLOIN STEAK 3.25
CLUB STEAK 2.75
COTTAGE FRIED STEAK 2.00
HAMBURGER STEAK 2.00
FILET MIGNON (wrapped in bacon) 3.75
TENDERLOIN STEAK 4.25
TENDERLOIN STEAK SANDWICH 2.50
LAMB CHOPS 2.85
PORK CHOPS 2.00

With the Above: Hashed Browned or French Fried Potatoes
Alvarado Special Tossed Salad, Rolls and Butter

Roy Williams, Manager   Tuesday, July 30th, 1957

PARKING AVAILABLE ONE BLOCK NORTH OR ACROSS THE STREET FROM HOTEL

• Approximately 3% State and City Sales Tax will be added to the above prices •

• Arrangements gladly made for special diet. Suggestions or criticisms regarding our service will be appreciated. We regret we cannot be responsible for the loss of wearing apparel or personal effects.

INDIAN BUILDING
FRED HARVEY

alvarado hotel & railroad depot

past

future

alvarado transportation center

Settlers trickled in from the East,

bearing bricks, clapboards and peaked roofs

to take root amongst the native rounded corners

and shaded *portales*.

Highrise now overlooks *hacienda*,

and asphalt blends with *adobe*.

91

And in just a few dazzling decades...

economic development and building booms.

Pushing the boundaries of the way things were

to the limits of the way things can be.

Library, University of New Mexico

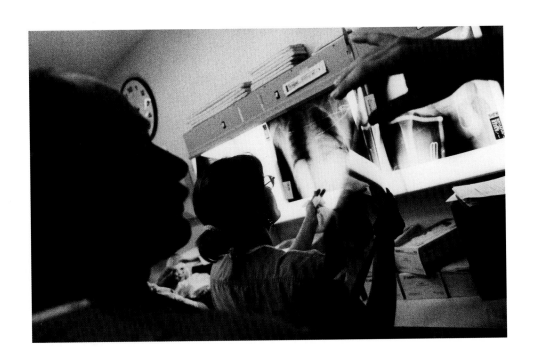

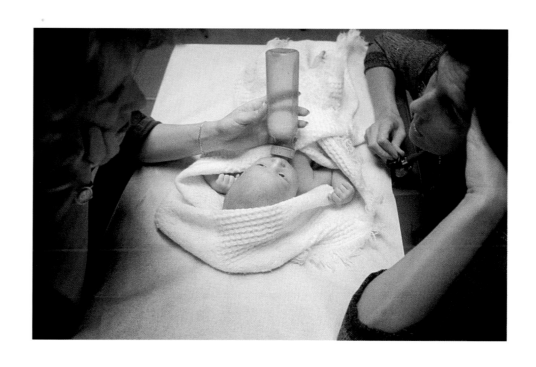

Central Avenue, Looking West

111

Boundless growth through boundless energy.

Stepping out in every direction...

establishing a toehold and moving on.

Sandia Peak and Needle, Sandia Mountains

ITALIAN MA
GUARANT
WHOLESAL
SANITARY BAKERY
SANITARY BAKERY
Siro Chiordi PROP.

Bernalillo County is a
celebration of coexistence.
A three-century evolution from
scattered farms and *ranchos* into
close communities sharing a
rich blend of ethnic cultures.
Here is pride in place, heritage and family.

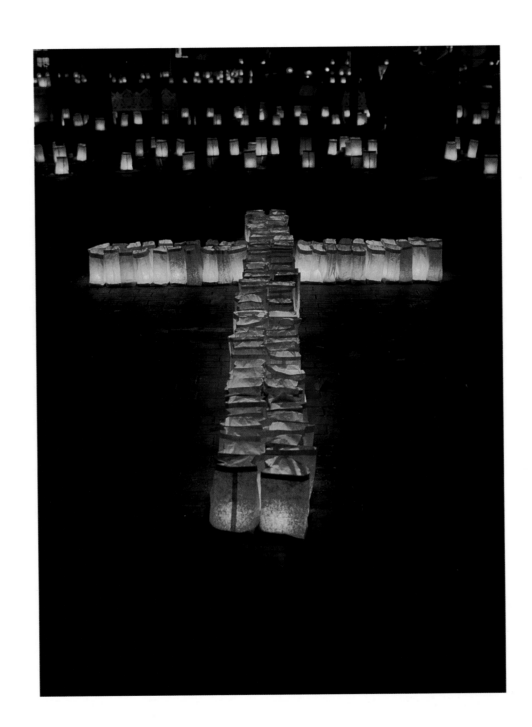

And tucked snugly away within the communities nestle neighborhoods that reveal smaller, more intimate *historias* of their own. Los Duranes. Barelas. Martineztown. Huning Highland. Signal Hill. Princess Jeanne. Trumbell. Los Ranchos. Corrales. Paradise Hills. Far more than the intersection of streets...this is the crossing of lives.

JOSEPH J. BA

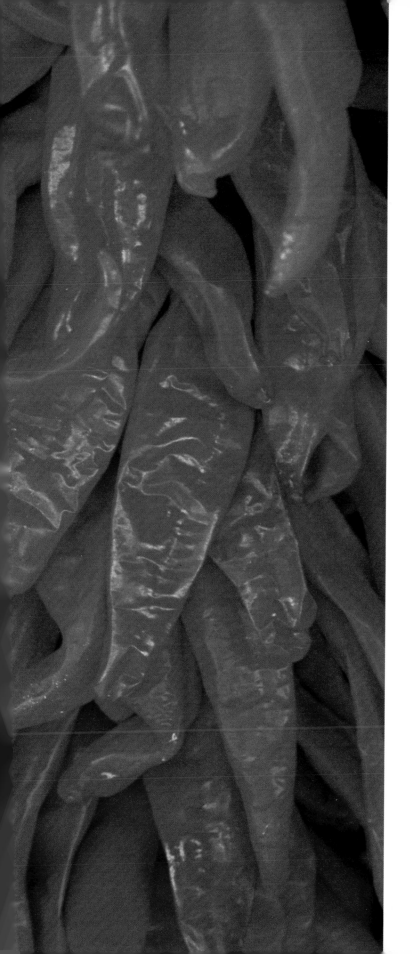

Of all life's questions
both great and small,
one towers high
above them all.

"Is there a heaven?"

"Has God been seen?"

No, dearest friends,
it's "Red or Green?"

translated from ancient Spanish proverb

It is the lives of its neighbors that gives a neighborhood its

vida. All the different faces, all the personal stories that

contribute to its unique personality. Friend and foe, famous

and infamous, they are the spice that sweetens the *olla*.

1
4
5

Albuquerque's diversity weaves a multi-colored, multi-textured cultural tapestry. The warp of many *tradiciónes* binds the weft of our festivals, celebrations, observances and rituals. Chinese New Year. Día de los Muertos. Juneteenth. The Gathering of Nations. The Greek Festival. We enjoy an embarrassment of riches.

153

The light of
creativity
shines brightly
here...and the
altitude removes
all limitations to
the reach of
inspiration.
Writers, artists,
musicians and
crafts persons
have long sought,
and received,
space for
reflection in the
nurturing
embrace of our
valley. The
mind soars
sín fronteras.

Navajo and Pueblo Indian Craftsmen, Silversmiths and Turquoise Drillers

PHOTO COURTESY MAISEL'S INDIAN TRADING POST

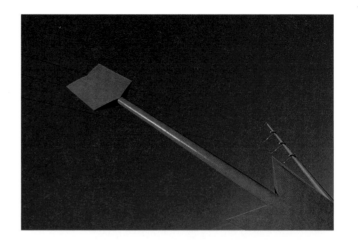

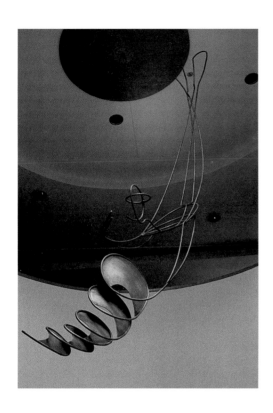

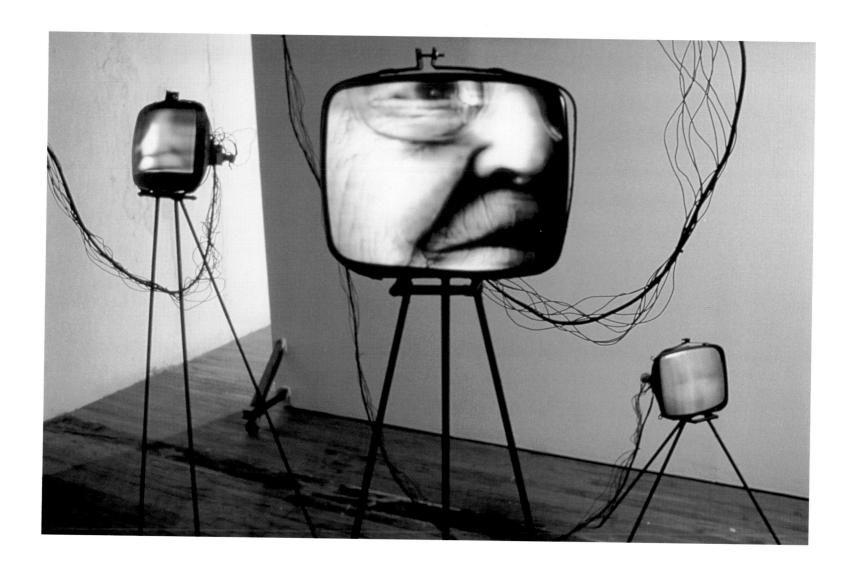

Boundless blue skies stretch a canopy of infinite possibilities across the high desert. Upon this canvas splashes the color riot of the Kodak™ Albuquerque International Balloon Fiesta and the New Mexico State Fair.

albuquerque's first balloon ascension

The Aquarium, Zoo and live concerts bask in our rarified glow.

And only the attraction of a legendary sports facility can draw one indoors.

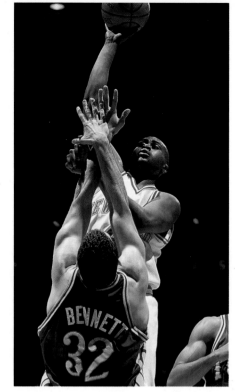

Within the dazzle of our azure aura beckons a rush of hiking, biking, skiing, rollerblading, jogging, golfing and horseback riding. Surely, there are no greater outdoors to be found anywhere.

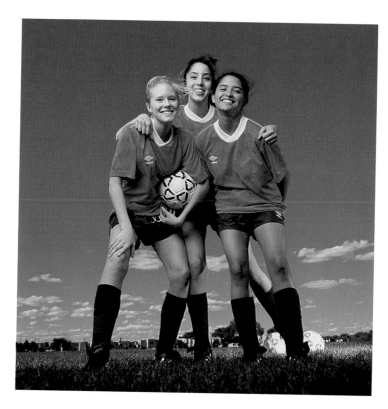

Grande meanders, the Sandias protect,

the mesa calms,

the volcanoes slumber.

Even as the urban landscape shifts,

the cottonwood's roots hold steadfast.

Mientras más cambian las cosas,

más se quedan igual.

The more things change,

the more they stay the same.

in the
spirit
of sponsorship:

AS REPRESENTATIVES OF THE REGION, THESE CORPORATIONS
BUSINESS ORGANIZATIONS AND EDUCATIONAL INSTITUTION
TAKE GREAT *ORGULLO* IN OUR PAST, PRESENT AND FUTURE...AN
IN OUR SHARED SPIRIT. THEIR INDIVIDUAL SUCCESS STORIE
ARE THE STORIES OF ALBUQUERQUE AND BERNALILLO COUNT

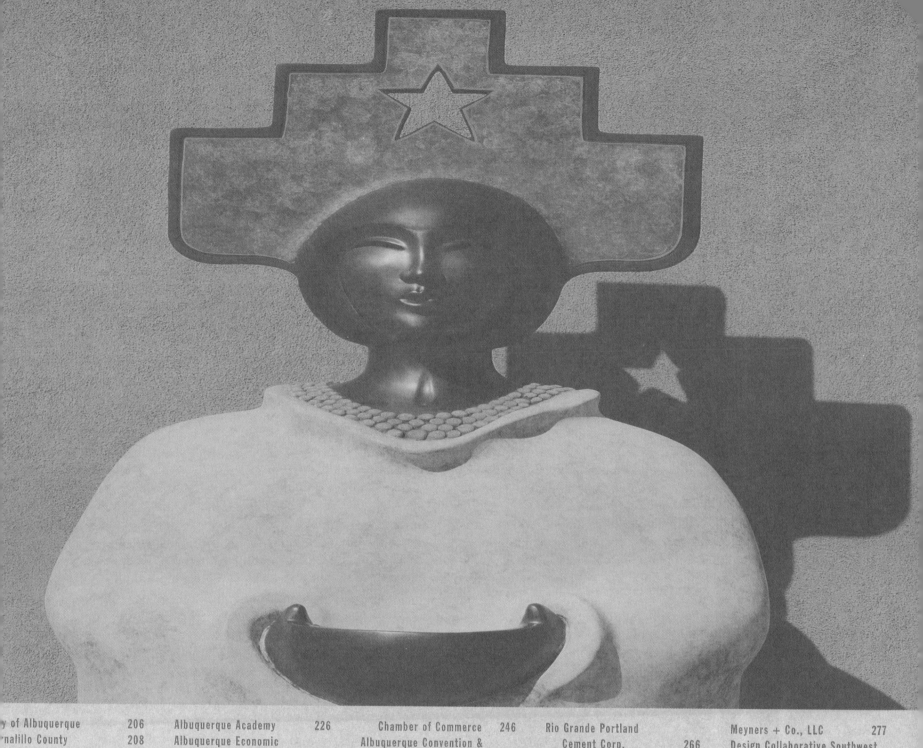

Cosmopolitan and casual, high-tech and heart-of-the-country, Albuquerque has a global economic presence and a hometown feel. "Albuquerque residents revel in their climate, their cultures, and their neighborhoods," says Mayor Jim Baca. "We continue to become a more sophisticated metropolitan hub, balancing our growth with our quality of life." A recent study by the Milken Institute of America's high-tech economy rated Albuquerque number one in the Top 50 High-Tech Metros, by growth, and seventh in their ranking of "Tech Poles" nationwide. Home to Sandia National Laboratories, Kirtland AFB and the Air Force Space Research Lab, Intel, Philips Semiconductors, Sumitomo Sitix, and the Science and Technology Center at the University of New Mexico, the Albuquerque area boasts a technology infrastructure that ranks among the world's best. These synergistic research opportunities are located in a setting of timeless beauty, where a rich history enlightens every corner.

The city's skilled work force and area employers are supported by Albuquerque's excellent Technical Vocational Institute (TVI), and an outstanding university and business school, the University of New Mexico and its Anderson School of Management. Albuquerque's public school system is far-reaching and comprehensive, and the city has some of the best private schools anywhere. "More and more young people are choosing to stay here for the educational and job opportunities we offer, especially in high-technology research and development and manufacturing," Mayor Baca notes. "Our economic development strategy is consciously based on developing diverse, high-tech clusters of employment for a broad cross-section of our residents."

Albuquerqueans reinvest in their city, supporting a strong downtown core where living and working coexist with an arts and entertainment hub and thriving tourism opportunities. Outlying neighborhoods blossom, each with its own

▶ The Albuquerque Convention Center welcomes thousands of visitors from around the world at this state-of-the-art facility.

2 0 6

Mayor Jim Baca heads his hometown and New Mexico's largest city, Albuquerque.

character and resources. Albuquerque is the heart of a region that recognizes that public concerns often cross political boundaries. Mayor Baca and the seven mayors of the other towns in the Middle Rio Grande basin meet as a forum to discuss air quality, water management, transportation and other issues. "We affect our neighbors. By planning together, we can build a positive future for the city and the region," says Mayor Baca. In this and similar efforts, the city provides strong leadership in regional affairs by pulling together ideas and resources from city, state and national resources.

The City of Albuquerque has a global presence and a hometown feel.

Albuquerque can mean many things to many people. In Albuquerque, "home" is townhouse, bungalow, hacienda, dorm room, farmhouse, base housing. The city's economic and cultural diversity is its strength. And while Albuquerque itself is "home" to major high-tech, research and educational institutions, it provides a strong community and an excellent quality of life to its residents. Local government and its leaders are working together to ensure a successful, sustainable future for all citizens. Our great natural landscape and wonderful climate provide stunning support to a dynamic modern city embodying the Spirit of the New West.

City of Albuquerque, One Civic Plaza NW, Albuquerque, NM 87102, 768-3000, www.cabq.gov

The Albuquerque Aquarium takes visitors on a fascinating journey through the marine habitats of the Gulf of Mexico.

the **spirit** of
BERNALILLO COUNTY est. 1844

As the new century unfolds, Bernalillo County is positioned to lead the way to a new era. With Albuquerque as the County seat, Bernalillo County has emerged as a center for culture, commerce and industry. Located in the middle of the stunning Rio Grande Valley, the area is rated as one of the nation's best for new business and development, advanced labor force and quality of life. Stretching across 1,200 square miles from the East Mountains just north of the Sandias to the majestic vistas of the West Side, more than half a million residents are living and working within its boundaries.

Technology is a stronghold in the business community with Sandia Laboratory at the core. Employing thousands, their mission is uniting science and engineering to serve important national needs. From defense technologies to energy and environment, the research and development taking place at Sandia Labs is actively providing solutions for government and industry. Several

businesses support this high-tech region with a strong and diversified work force.

The University of New Mexico has more than 30,000 students enrolled in undergraduate programs and offers bachelor's degrees in several accredited disciplines ranging from business to science. The University of New Mexico School of Medicine has received national recognition for many of its programs and the Clinical Law School at the University is rated one of the best in the nation. Albuquerque Technical Vocational Institute works closely with local industries to continually assess and create programs needed in an ever-changing technical environment. A Workforce Training Center will soon be completed and can efficiently coordinate curriculum with industry needs.

Bernalillo County is strategically situated and easily accessible. Hundreds of flights per day arrive and depart from the Albuquerque International Sunport. Ground transportation includes two major interstates, I-25 and I-40, designed to handle large volumes of traffic and a railway system with connections throughout the country. Strong ties to Central and South America makes this area a perfect choice for trade opportunities. Bernalillo County's prime location promotes NAFTA objectives of trade and commerce.

▶ Bernalillo County's newest community center, Vista Grande, is situated in the East Mountains with the National Forest as a backdrop. The centers serve an ever-growing community by offering a wide variety of youth, adult and senior programs.

An early 1900s church now serves as a jointly operated senior center for Bernalillo County. Adorning the front of the renovated Pajarito Senior Center is "The Settler," by artist Esteban Duran, a formation in tin showing the historic significance and contributions of early farmers.

Bernalillo County Government is a strong supporter of new business and economic development. Working closely with other government agencies, Industrial Revenue Bonds can be issued, allowing exemptions from property taxes and gross receipts taxes on equipment purchases. State officials recently granted authority to begin the process of local government unification and for the creation of a metropolitan utility service.

Immersed in cultural diversity, Bernalillo County offers rich history carefully preserved through architecture, community celebrations and social attitudes. A mild climate boasting a spectrum of seasons, affordable housing, a clean environment, low personal and property taxes, a

Bernalillo County is rated as one of the nation's best for quality of life.

low unemployment rate and professional sports all contribute to the already inviting and warm atmosphere.

Since its inception, the County has been a guiding force for progress in New Mexico. Bernalillo County is dedicated to a commitment of progress, financial stability, planned growth and economic development while providing a quality of life for residents.

Office of Econ. Development, One Civic Plaza NW, 10th Floor, Albuquerque, NM 87102, 768-4000, www.bernco.gov

Bernalillo County's "1% for Arts" program has provided art pieces throughout the county, including Reynaldo "Sonny" Rivera's "Mimo y Los Tres Niños," a bronze sculpture capturing a playful childhood moment, in front of the South Valley Library.

the **spirit** of
JOURNAL PUBLISHING COMPANY est. 1880

As New Mexico's oldest and largest newspaper, the *Albuquerque Journal* not only keeps the state's citizens informed, it keeps them connected. Tracing its roots back to 1880, the newspaper has always been a forum for public debate and a conduit for information, providing news coverage on important issues throughout the city, state and country.

▶ **Albuquerque Journal's downtown office in 1985.**

The *Journal* is home to some of the state's best-known journalists, including columnists Jim Belshaw and Larry Calloway, and cartoonist John Trever, whose unique style of political cartoons has graced the *Journal*'s pages for more than 22 years. And the *Journal*'s desks – which cover everything from state and national news to business to arts to trends to sports – keep readers abreast of a wide variety of issues.

T.H. Lang, president and publisher.

The newspaper prides itself on keeping up with the latest technology and providing a vast array of services to its readers. The *Journal*'s website hosts more than 6,000 pages of news, features and information content, as well as on-line advertising for readers. In print the *Journal* puts out four editions a day – making sure readers have up-to-date information on the latest events.

The *Journal* is published by the Journal Publishing Co., headed by brothers T.H. and W.P. Lang. T.H. Lang, president/publisher, has a long-standing interest in the state. An Albuquerque native who attended UNM, T.H. Lang has been at the helm of the *Journal* since 1971. He has expanded the newspaper's presence throughout New Mexico and established *Journal* bureaus in Santa Fe, Las Cruces and Washington, D.C. In addition to the four basic editions, the newspaper also publishes zoned news and advertising sections emphasizing different regions, including *Journal North*, covering the state Capitol and northern New

210

Mexico; the *West Side Journal*, covering Rio Rancho and the metro area's West Side; *Journal South*, covering Valencia County; and the *Mountain View Journal*, focusing on the East Mountains and Torrance County. "The *Journal* has always been the newspaper of record for the state, and I want our coverage and reach to live up to that," Lang says.

A home-owned and home-operated newspaper – a rarity in today's group-dominated media industry – the *Journal* has a strong commitment to give back to the community. It has awarded approximately $450,000 in college scholarships since 1984 and sponsored many events, seminars, fairs and other activities aimed at supporting charitable organizations and causes. The Lang family also has developed Journal Center, a Class-A office and industrial park off of north I-25. "We are committed to participate in the ongoing progress and promise of New Mexico and Albuquerque," T.H. Lang says.

"The Journal has always been the newspaper of record for the state."

7777 Jefferson Boulevard NE, Albuquerque, NM 87109, 823-7777, www.ABQjournal.com

Albuquerque Journal's current location at Journal Center.

The people, programs and places of the University of New Mexico are unsurpassed in the state as a source of educational enrichment and renewal. With more than 24,200 students on the main campus and another 6,700 at its branches, 92,000 alumni (52,600 in New Mexico), 1,669 full-time faculty members, and more than 7,000 full-time staff, UNM is a pool of diverse talent.

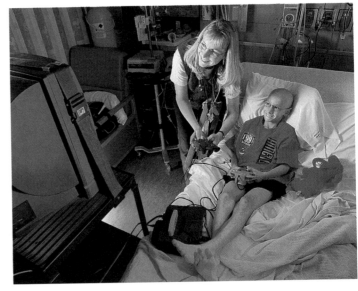

A pediatrician and faculty member from the UNM School of Medicine visits a young cancer patient in Children's Hospital of New Mexico. CHNM is a component of the Health Sciences Center.

Outstanding programs offered under the auspices of UNM's top ranked schools and colleges include traditional and innovative courses in the Schools of Law, Medicine, Architecture and Planning, Engineering, the College of Arts and Sciences, and the Anderson Schools of Management, among others. UNM has a statewide presence at its main campus in Albuquerque, which includes the Health Sciences Center, and in Los Alamos, Taos, Valencia County, Santa Fe and Gallup. As University President William C. Gordon puts it, "Today UNM connects with virtually all citizens in the state through courses they take, the health care they receive, the recreational and cultural activities they enjoy, and research that has contributed to their daily lives."

UNM researchers Terry Yates and Cheryl Parmenter examine samples from their work on the Hantavirus. UNM, a Carnegie I University, is the state's largest university, with a commitment to multicultural education service and research programs.

UNM, through the efforts of its outstanding faculty, has garnered academic recognition in all phases of achievement. In 1998–1999, the clinical law training program moved ahead of Ivy League schools to number five in the nation, and the graduate program at UNM's School of Engineering was listed in the Top 50, according to *U.S. News & World Report*. UNM was awarded a total of $218.6 million in grants and contracts for areas such as Research, Public Service, Instruction and Financial Aid in fiscal year 1999. Of that total, $148.7 million was brought in by the Main Campus, while $70 million was brought in by the Health Sciences Center.

The Health Sciences Center at UNM is a vital and viable proving ground for new medicine and methodologies, and the School of Medicine was ranked in the Top 10 Best Medical Colleges by *U.S. News & World Report*. The Health Sciences Center encompasses the School of Medicine, the College of Nursing, the College of Pharmacy, the Health

Sciences Center Library and six clinical facilities, including University Hospital. Biomedical research at UNM contributes cutting-edge scientific information that is applied to clinical practice, enhances educational opportunities, improves patient care and solves health-care problems facing New Mexico. In 1997 University Hospital and the School of Medicine created the UNM Care Plan for the uninsured of Bernalillo County, a new program adopted as a model by other institutions of health-care. UNM's patient initiatives also include new models developed for community-based health care in rural communities, to integrate interdisci-plinary services, and create common health-care goals and priorities. In 1998 the Health Sciences Center represented

> UNM connects with citizens statewide through
> education, health care, culture and research.

48 percent of UNM's budget, employed more than 6,000 faculty and staff, educated 2,200 students, served 117,000 patients, and logged 641,610 ambulatory care clinic visits statewide.

The University of New Mexico's dedicated people, innovative programs and statewide presence put it in a special class in terms of educational opportunities, research, health care and community service.

UNM, Public Affairs Office, 2nd Floor, Hodgin Hall, Albuquerque NM 87131, 277-5813, www.unm.edu

UNM's unique campus features buildings and facilities constructed in the Spanish Pueblo Revival. The newest is a state-of-the-art classroom building, Dane Smith Hall.

the spirit of
ST. JOSEPH HEALTHCARE est. 1902

A spirit of innovation, a legacy of care. This simple motto characterizes the nearly 100 years St. Joseph Healthcare has proudly served Albuquerque. SJH was founded in Albuquerque in 1902 by the Sisters of Charity. Intent on meeting the needs of the fledgling community, the Sisters made it their mission to care for the poor and under-served.

Today SJH is part of a bigger system, Catholic Health Initiatives, the largest faith-based, not-for-profit health-care system in the nation.

St. Joseph Healthcare's main campus lies downtown in the heart of the city's historical district. Inside the elegant brownstone building now known as St. Joseph Square, a nationally registered historical landmark, and the accompanying Medical Center, is evidence of the cutting-edge technology and forward-thinking philosophy SJH has made the hallmark of its commitment to providing the best care in New Mexico.

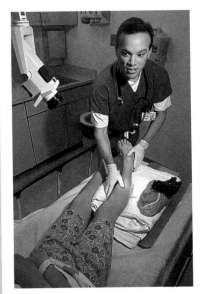

In 1999 St. Joseph Healthcare was named one of the nation's 100 most "techno-savvy healthcare systems" by *Hospital and Health Networks* magazine. SJH's significant investment in an integrated health information system ensures that physicians have the most sophisticated medical information available while maintaining accurate, updated patient records capable of cross-checking for such details as drug interaction warnings, lab results or health plan restrictions. SJH's website at www.sjhs.org, in conjunction with AmericasDoctor.com, offers easily accessible, reliable health information via on-line, real-time chats with physicians and an extensive medical library.

St. Joseph Healthcare's partnership in another state-of-the art enterprise, the Heart Hospital of New Mexico, further exemplifies its commitment to providing high-tech yet compassionate care. The Heart Hospital, a joint venture with New Mexico Heart Institute, Southwest Cardiology and MedCath, Inc., is the state's first specialty hospital focused on the treatment of heart disease. Its patient-centered design includes all private rooms designed to function at every level of care, 24-hour visiting hours, sleeper beds for family members and around-the-clock, in-room meals for patients and their visitors.

St. Joseph Healthcare counts several other firsts, including St. Joseph West Mesa Hospital, with the only full-service emergency room complete with board-certified ER physicians on Albuquerque's West Side. St. Joseph MedicarePlus, a health plan for Medicare-eligible individuals, is the state's first provider-sponsored organization. St. Joseph Regional Cancer Center, coming to the St. Joseph Northeast Heights Hospital campus next spring, will be the first patient-focused, "one-stop shop" giving cancer patients access to doctors and specialists at one time, in one location. Other SJH programs and services include St. Joseph Eye Surgery Center, St. Joseph Rehabilitation Hospital & Outpatient Center, St. Joseph Physician Group, St. Joseph Sleep Diagnostic Center, St. Joseph Women's Care and St. Joseph Senior Care.

St. Joseph is dedicated to providing for patients — body, mind and spirit.

St Joseph Healthcare is poised to celebrate the start of its next 100 years by providing advanced health-care services with the same compassion that the Sisters of Charity brought to New Mexico nearly a century ago.

7850 Jefferson Boulevard NE, Albuquerque, NM 87109, 727-8000, www.sjhs.org

St. Joseph Medical Center today sits on the same spot where the Sisters of Charity built "St. Jospeh Sanatorium" — Albuquerque's first hospital.

the Spirit of
PRESBYTERIAN HEALTHCARE SERVICES est. 1908

Continuous investment in technology and a commitment to patient-centered care has made Presbyterian New Mexico's leader in heart care — and one of the nation's top heart care centers.

The history and future of Presbyterian are reflected in the life story of Mrs. Van, whose legacy of caring guides the organization today.

From humble beginnings at the dawn of the century, Presbyterian Healthcare Services has grown into the region's leading health-care provider.

In the early 1900s, Albuquerque was a small-town haven for tuberculosis patients. In those days it was thought that the arid New Mexico climate provided the perfect environment for healing. One such patient, the Rev. Hugh A. Cooper, was more fortunate than most and regained his health rather quickly after coming to town. In 1908 he founded the Southwestern Presbyterian Sanatorium, a facility whose sole purpose was to care for the hundreds of TB patients coming to the city.

That was over 90 years ago. Today, thanks to an enduring commitment to world-class medicine and compassionate patient care, Presbyterian Healthcare Services is poised to continue its mission to improve the health of New Mexicans into the next century. As the

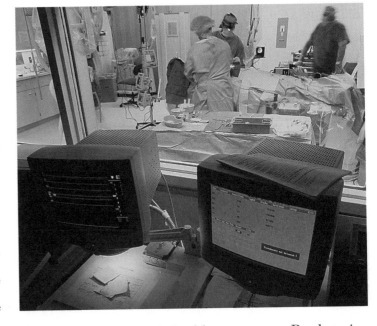

state's only locally headquartered, not-for-profit health-care system, Presbyterian is also one of the state's largest employers. Presbyterian Health Plan cares for over 330,000 members, making it the largest health plan in the state. In 1968 the state's first heart center was born at Presbyterian Hospital, and now ranks among the top 100 nationwide for positive patient outcomes and value.

No matter how much Presbyterian has grown, however, our guiding principles have remained steadfast. Over the past 90 years our organization has been fortunate enough to attract a seemingly unending supply of caring professionals who've dedicated themselves to improving the health of those they are privileged to serve. One such person was the late Marion Kellogg Van Devanter.

Arriving in Albuquerque in the spring of 1921, Marion's only intention was to visit her fiancé, a tuberculosis patient by the name of Jimmy Van Devanter. She ended up spending the next 63 years of her life here, selflessly serving our patients in every way imaginable. Today, her spirit is embodied and carried on by the many Presbyterian physicians, nurses and staff who honor her memory with compassionate care. Mrs. Van's legacy also lives on in our 25-member volunteer board of directors, who strive to remain humble in their role as stewards of New Mexico's health-care resources. Perhaps that's one reason why Presbyterian has received the Consumer's Choice Award for four consecutive years and has been consistently recognized as Albuquerque's best hospital, best family health-care provider and best health-care organization.

Over the decades, Presbyterian has been a nationally recognized health care provider.

Our past has taught us that in the coming years the challenges within health care will continue to evolve. Yet the overall purpose of Presbyterian will always remain the same: to improve the health of the individuals, families and communities we serve. Now and in the future.

5901 Harper Drive NE, Albuquerque, NM 87109, 260-6307, www.phs.org

From humble beginnings in 1908, Presbyterian has grown into the state's largest health plan, most advanced hospital and leading heart care provider.

From business club to catalyst for economic opportunity, the Greater Albuquerque Chamber of Commerce has grown along with the Albuquerque metropolitan area to become a primary resource for and advocate of commerce and industry in New Mexico.

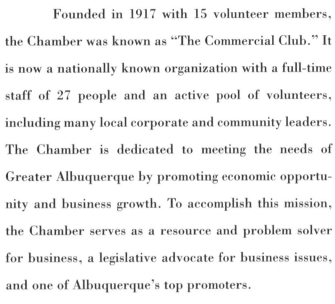

▶

The GACC provides many informative seminars, networking opportunities and membership events to its member organizations.

Founded in 1917 with 15 volunteer members, the Chamber was known as "The Commercial Club." It is now a nationally known organization with a full-time staff of 27 people and an active pool of volunteers, including many local corporate and community leaders. The Chamber is dedicated to meeting the needs of Greater Albuquerque by promoting economic opportunity and business growth. To accomplish this mission, the Chamber serves as a resource and problem solver for business, a legislative advocate for business issues, and one of Albuquerque's top promoters.

With 3,200 member organizations, the Chamber is in the business of raising the standard of living for all people. By bringing together businesses of all sizes, the Chamber is able to increase sustainable, quality growth. Through key relationships with major area institutions like Sandia National Laboratories/Lockheed Martin, Kirtland Air Force Base, the University of New Mexico and Intel, the Chamber is a leader in fostering technology growth in Albuquerque.

One of the Chamber's top priorities is education reform. "Our education efforts directly affect our quality of life," says Adelmo "Del" Archuleta, 1999–2000 Chairman of the Board. "We are working to make positive public school education reform a reality here in Albuquerque, the result of which will be a educational system which is second to none. Our goals include every student reading at grade level and graduating ready for college or the work force."

The Chamber believes that work-force development begins in school and is committed to reforming public education. "Our goal is consistently strong education throughout the system. We want every student to have the same opportunities and expectations regardless of their demographics or economic status," says Chamber President Terri Cole, CCE. The Chamber has developed several programs to help students and educators, including Youth Leadership, which fosters leadership capabilities in Albuquerque's youth, and other programs which recognize outstanding students and teachers.

The Chamber is also a catalyst for change in regard to regional issues such as economic development, water and land use, transportation, air quality, telecommunications and health care. Regional growth is rapid, and this growth is creating major issues for Albuquerqueans and their neighbors. By supporting such area initiatives as a regional transportation authority, water conservation and management, revitalization of the city's downtown, and the master-planned development of Albuquerque's burgeoning West Side, the Chamber helps city leaders deal with their most pressing concerns. "At no time in Albuquerque's history has it been more critical to plan for our future," says Terri Cole. "We need to make some important decisions on a regional level, decisions that affect New Mexico as a place to live, raise a family and be in business."

The Chamber serves as a resource and a problem solver for the city of Albuquerque.

As Albuquerque stands on the brink of the new millennium, it is positioned for an unprecedented era of growth and development. The Chamber of Commerce will stand side by side with the business community to foster regional cooperation, economic opportunity and quality of life in Albuquerque and throughout New Mexico.

401 2nd Street NW, Albuquerque, NM 87102, 764-3700, www.gacc.org

From left: Rick Alvidrez is GACC's 1999–2000 Chairman-Elect and an attorney with Keleher and McLeod, PA. Terri Cole, CCE, is the President of GACC and Adelmo "Del" Archuleta is the 1999–2000 Chairman of the Board and the CEO of Molzen-Corbin Associates architectural firm.

There's a lot of change going on these days at Public Service Company of New Mexico – or "PNM," as the local folks call it. Yes, the company is seeing some serious *movimiento*.

The company that has provided electric and gas services to hundreds of thousands of New Mexicans since 1917 – and was the first New Mexico–based company listed on the New York Stock Exchange – is reinventing itself for a deregulated electric marketplace.

> PNM's statewide customer call center offers expanded hours, from 7am–9pm weekdays, and Saturdays from 9am–3pm for more convenience.

PNM will continue to deliver electricity to homes and businesses throughout its electric service territory, which includes 360,000 customers in Albuquerque, Santa Fe, Las Vegas, Belen, Clayton and Deming. On any given summer afternoon, these customers use about 1,300 megawatts of electricity, or the equivalent of 13 million 100-watt bulbs, all lit simultaneously.

But where the power comes from – where it is generated – will change. New Mexico has an electric utility deregulation law, passed in 1999, that gives customers a choice of where they buy power beginning in

> Once customers have a choice of electric suppliers, PNM's dependable system will deliver power supply to homes and businesses.

2001. This creates a great challenge for PNM: how to make customer choice really work.

In the coming months and years, PNM will work actively to educate customers about their options and to make the transition to this new era as smooth as possible. Meanwhile, PNM will strengthen the commitment to community, the environment and its work force that already makes it a real force in Albuquerque's economy.

With 2,800 employees throughout New Mexico, PNM is an employer of some of the community's most promising workers. And the company remains committed to the city and its roots. In 1999 *Fortune* named PNM the best place in America for Hispanics to work. Similarly, *Computerworld* in 1999 named PNM as one of the 100 best companies nationwide for employees who are information professionals.

The company is a standout in the environmental area as well. Its avian program, designed to prevent raptors from being injured or killed by power lines, has earned the company a Conservation Service Award from U.S. Secretary of the Interior Bruce Babbitt. And, PNM has received state and regional recognition for its tree-trimming practices to clean trees from power lines.

Similarly, the company developed the TAMIS™ software system that allows line maintenance crews with laptop computers to quickly identify access routes that avoid archeological sites and environmentally sensitive areas. This system also speeds up crews' response times to power line or equipment problems.

Above all, PNM remains committed to its 1.3 million electric and gas customers throughout New Mexico. PNM knows the important role it plays in keeping homes comfortable and businesses operating at productive levels.

That's why keeping the lights on and the gas flowing remain PNM's highest priorities – and why affordability is never far behind. Until 2001, thanks to a $34 million agreement PNM helped create, residential and small business customers will buy electricity at the lowest rates since 1985.

PNM knows that as Albuquerque grows, the demand for reliable, affordable electric and gas services will, too. That's why PNM's work today focuses on tomorrow's needs and tomorrow's demands.

Amid all of this *movimiento*, some things will never change. And that's something Albuquerque can be proud of.

PNM, Alvarado Square, Albuquerque, NM 87158, 241-2700, www.pnm.com

> PNM's work today focuses on tomorrow's needs and tomorrow's demands.

PNM spends more than $100 million a year maintaining and improving its electric system.

Nurturing, stewardship and fun are not the usual words we think of when we think of a bank. The world of high finance seems far-removed from the everyday lives of children, who, after all, are not the bank's prime customers. But a company with deep roots in its community knows that the questions of the future can be answered in the shaping of just one child's present. At First State Bank, they invest in the future of New Mexico's children.

Members of senior management show the fun side of banking at First State Bank.

First State Bank's open-handed giving accrues with the time and effort that executives and employees alike give to non-profit organizations and events that benefit children. Their work for New Mexico Children First, ChildRite, United Way, Habitat for Humanity, and New Mexico Children's Foundation, among other charities, reflects the bank's deep emphasis on the needs of children and their families. "Problems start in childhood, and can be solved in childhood," says First State president Mike Stanford. "We're part of that solution." To achieve that worthwhile goal, the company supports organizations that provide the important basics, like immunization, nourishment, housing and education, to the state's neediest children.

Helping New Mexico's children grow up to be healthy, happy adults mirrors First State's view that businesses, large and small, need nurturing, too. For this bank, economic opportunity and growth begins at home, with a vital employee population and a climate that allows companies to flourish. First State has been a New Mexico bank since it began in Taos in 1922, and has itself grown large enough to handle the financial needs of any size of business. A home-grown bank with a small-town feel, First State also offers customers access to the latest on-line banking technology. You might want to visit a nearby branch, however, to sample the welcoming warmth and sense of place that is their local trademark. But don't feel you have to dress up – come as you are, in a business suit or workday denim, and have fun while you bank in First State's friendly surroundings.

First State's community relationships are enriched by its work on behalf of New Mexico's children, and by the ties its people maintain with other groups that contribute to the quality of life here. Leadership New Mexico, the Jewish Foundation, Kirtland Partnership and the Greater Albuquerque Chamber of Commerce are just a few of the organizations that have profited from the involvement of First State employees on their boards and committees. First State employees generate the spirit, the energy and the wherewithal to support the endeavors of the American Cancer Society, the Nike Tour and the March of Dimes, acting locally to enhance the community-at-large.

New Mexico's rich tri-cultural heritage is reflected in the diversity among First State's employees and customers. Truly a New Mexico institution, this bank is uniquely positioned and solidly grounded in the community it serves. First State's commitment to children in their present and future lives speaks to the company's constantly renewed and revitalizing faith in New Mexico and hope for its families. After all, First State's employees have more than 300 children of their own.

PO Box 3686, Albuquerque, NM 87190, 241-7500, www.fsbnm.com

> **First State's commitment to children speaks to its hope for New Mexico's families.**

Some of the Albuquerque employees and family members pose in front of First State's newest office at 8100 Lang Avenue NE.

Sandia Laboratory Federal Credit Union is a unique source of high value, custom-designed and closely supported high-technology financial services. Unique, because of the level of trust members have in their credit union as a safe and familiar place to save and a reliable and low-cost place to borrow. Unique, too, because membership in SLFCU is a value-added employee benefit that costs employers nothing.

SLFCU was founded in 1948, by and for the employees of the country's premier national scientific laboratory. It now serves over 42,000 members through a growing list of employers. SLFCU specifically seeks employers in high-technology fields who wish to offer their employees the services one of the leading credit unions in the United States. Based on 1998 financial reports, SLFCU ranked 103 by asset size among 11,658 U.S. credit unions. And SLFCU has consistently ranked among the top credit unions in the U.S. in total Return to Members, a measure that includes high savings rates, low loan rates, low or no fees, and high member acceptance of products and services.

▶ Friendly, knowledgeable Phone Center personnel provide account information, answer questions and make loans.

Those products and services set a high standard for value. SLFCU members benefit from convenient, interest-bearing checking accounts, market-leading savings accounts and certificates, a full-service Financial Center, low-cost loans, and credit and debit cards accepted worldwide. Members use their credit union day and night from work, home or while traveling through a professionally staffed, toll-free Phone

To President/CEO Chris Jillson, personal service to members is what sets SLFCU apart from its competition.

Center, free CU@home® computer home banking, and CUROS® automated telephone teller.

Technology promises efficiency and convenience in many forms to every financial organization, but the most effective technologies are coupled with the highest levels of service quality. SLFCU members and their employers can

224

be confident that their credit union will maintain its focus on member service and its keen technological edge. The SLFCU management team and board make informed operational decisions from strategic plans driven by member expectations, not by quarterly profit projections, takeover fears and transitory business pressures. As banks are swallowed by unfamiliar rivals – as the financial marketplace undergoes dramatic change – SLFCU members will continue to enjoy top returns and the highest quality of service.

It's a forecast based on a well-documented track record. For safety, soundness and high value, Sandia Laboratory Federal Credit Union has an impressive history of top ratings from federal examiners and industry analysts. Maintaining that position is a challenge SLFCU will meet in partnership with the credit union's fine group of high-technology employers, with Sandia National Laboratories at its core.

3707 Juan Tabo Boulevard NE, Albuquerque, NM 87111, 293-0500, 800-94-SLFCU, www.slfcu.org

> **SLFCU will maintain its focus on member service and its keen technological edge.**

Busy members have access to almost every SLFCU service through their home or office computer.

225

Academically rigorous, culturally and economically diverse, Albuquerque Academy is an independent, college preparatory day school for boys and girls in grades six through twelve. Situated on a scenic 312-acre campus, the Academy serves its students through exceptional course offerings. The breadth of academic experience at Albuquerque Academy is matched by the mastery of its teachers, carefully chosen from all over the world for their qualities as exceptional role models for children.

▶ The central campus walkway.

Founded in 1955 as a school for boys, Albuquerque Academy has seen remarkable growth thanks to the generosity of Albert G. Simms, a New Mexico financier and rancher, and his wife, Ruth Hanna McCormick Simms. Between 1957 and 1964, the Simms gifted a large tract of undeveloped land to the Academy. Sale of the land over the years and careful management of the proceeds have created a $200 million endowment which today enables Albuquerque Academy to provide students with the highest quality education.

The Academy's state-of-the-art natatorium opened in 1997. It features a competition pool and a multi-purpose pool with a movable fiberglass swim wall and a diving well.

Unique in the independent school world, the Academy's need-blind admission policy offers admission to qualified students regardless of their ability to pay. Only after students have been chosen are their tuition needs assessed and financial aid offered. Approximately 32 percent of Academy students receive need-based financial aid totaling upwards of $2.5 million each year.

Albuquerque Academy has a highly talented, motivated and diverse student body, 50 percent boys and 50 percent girls. Students come from throughout the greater Albuquerque area, and one-third are students of color. The student faculty ratio is 8:1, the average class size is 14, and more than 80 percent of the faculty hold advanced degrees.

The academic program in grades six and seven is interdisciplinary, and student life embraces a family model with a faculty advisor for every group of 10 students. Within the structure of a traditional curriculum, students in grades eight through twelve form appropriate bonds with teachers and advisors who nurture their educational development. Each student's particular passion translates into involvement in a wide range of extracurricular activities and athletics.

With the 1999 renovation of the Albert G. and Ruth Hanna McCormick Simms Center for the Performing Arts, the Academy completed a decade-long building program which included construction of a library, science center, nine-lane track, 16 tennis courts, music building and natatorium, as well as the refurbishment of classrooms. A required outdoor education program for students in grades six through ten takes place on the Academy's 270-acre Bear Canyon tract in the Sandia Mountains and at other sites throughout the state.

The Academy offers admission to qualified students regardless of their ability to pay.

Academy graduates have an enviable record of admittance to colleges and universities, assisted by the school's college placement office. In 1998–1999, Academy students took 300 Advanced Placement exams, with 90 percent earning college credits. Academy alumni, just over 3,000 in number, affirm the school's mission by demonstrating achievement, leadership and distinction in their professional and personal lives. They are, in the words of the Academy mission, "serving their communities with wisdom and conviction, and their fellow beings with compassion."

6400 Wyoming Boulevard NE, Albuquerque, NM 87109, 828-3200, www.aa.edu

Academy students in all grades participate in a wide range of visual and performing arts activities.

There are dramatic changes ahead for the domestic and global economies as we witness an accelerated transition to a new information-based economy. This transformation requires access to the best minds and talent that can apply creative new solutions to developing business opportunities. The world will reward the leaders in innovation and

▶ A contained group of high-rise buildings characterizes Albuquerque's downtown business district, providing a contrast to the low-land sprawl of the mesa to the west and the Rio Grande which slices the city.

technology advancement. Knowledge workers will make a difference in determining which communities prosper.

This shift benefits Albuquerque and Albuquerque Economic Development. As Randolph Court of the Progressive Policy Institute said, "New Mexico has a very high innovative capacity. And innovation really is the key to economic growth in the new economy." Albuquerque Economic Development will be central to that change, recruiting the select industries and companies of the future to invest in the Albuquerque metropolitan area. AED's mission is to stimulate the development of this new economy locally, building on our unique intellectual capital assets at Sandia National Laboratories, the Air Force Laboratories–Phillips Site, the University of New Mexico, Los Alamos National Laboratory and in other local institutions and companies.

The Sandia Peak Tram travels to the top of the 10,378-foot Sandia Peak, providing viewers 2.7 miles of changing life zones, and 11,000 square miles of panoramic views from the peak.

AED has played an important role in driving the development of the local and state economies since the organization was formed 40 years ago. According to the respected Milken Institute, the Albuquerque economy is now the fastest-growing high-tech metropolitan area in the United States. This ranking was achieved in part due to the leadership of several companies recruited by AED, including Intel, Philips Semiconductor, Honeywell and Sumitomo Sitix Silicon.

When AlliedSignal chose to launch its innovative Power Systems subsidiary, AED worked closely to provide site selection support to locate both the headquarters and initial production facility here, creating high-quality jobs for area residents.

AED will always be at the forefront, working to build a vibrant economic future. AED's success is dependent upon its many public and private sector partners, including the 350 businesses that are members of this non-profit organization. Their investment is important to Albuquerque's long-term economic health, building on a foundation of innovation.

AED's mission is to stimulate development of a local, information-based economy.

851 University Boulevard SE, Suite 203, Albuquerque, NM 87106, 246-6200, www.abq.org

The evening lights of the city glitter in the clear desert air.

Engineering and architecture isn't about roads, water and sewer systems, treatment plants and buildings – it's about people. This baseline philosophy is embedded in the firm's culture, as it has been since 1960, and guides day to day

life at Molzen-Corbin & Associates in working with communities throughout New Mexico. "We want to make the quality of life better for people – we take care of our clients," says Del Archuleta, Chief Executive Officer of Molzen-Corbin & Associates. "We are truly connected to the people whose lives we're improving – they can always rely on us."

Offering a full scope of multidiscipline services, Molzen-Corbin & Associates is recognized as a cutting-edge leader in cleaning up the state's water as a result of the 1972 Clean Water Act. In fact, one would be hard-pressed to find any other firm who has had such a dynamic, significant effect in ensuring safe drinking water for its citizens, as well as ensuring that treated wastewater returned to New Mexico's rivers and streams is of the highest purity. Through the

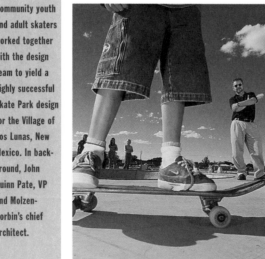

years, the firm's pioneering designs in water resources have been lauded through prestigious national and state awards.

Equally recognized for its strength in transportation and urban engineering, Molzen-Corbin has been pivotal in the development of the state's lifeline transportation network. They have designed enough highways, streets and roads to span New Mexico, along with runways and taxiways at major international and municipal airports extending into all four corners of the state.

Archuleta, who first joined the company as a young engineer out of New Mexico State University, quickly moved through the ranks as he set the pace for Molzen-Corbin's dynamic staff of engineers and architects. Under his leadership, Molzen-Corbin has been the City of Albuquerque's choice for engineering at its airport – for everything from runway improvements to design of the new Sunport Boulevard – to designing numerous water resources improvements

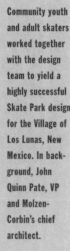

Molzen-Corbin & Associates boldly took on leadership in ensuring that New Mexico communities have safe drinking water. (from left) CEO Adelmo (Del) Archuleta with VPs Eric Sorenson, chief electrical engineer, and Ron Mosher, chief water resources engineer.

Community youth and adult skaters worked together with the design team to yield a highly successful Skate Park design for the Village of Los Lunas, New Mexico. In background, John Quinn Pate, VP and Molzen-Corbin's chief architect.

at the City's Southside Water Reclamation Plant, and the state-of-the-art Soils Amendment Facility, one of the premier composting facilities in the nation.

In addition to high-profile work in Albuquerque, the firm has continuously sustained the infrastructure development of the many cities surrounding the greater metropolitan area for the past four decades. Again, guided by an unwavering commitment to improve the quality of life, they have designed countless new water and wastewater treatment plants, better roads and drainage systems, hundreds of miles of water and sewer lines, as well as designed city halls, libraries, community centers, and recreation and park facilities.

> "We are connected to the people whose lives we're improving – they can always rely on us."

Be it New Mexico's metropolitan, urban or rural communities with which it has worked over the past 40 years, Molzen-Corbin & Associates brings relentless energy, dedication and uncompromised quality to each and every project. "Being an advocate for our clients and working with them hand in hand to face challenges and to find solutions for a better future is what Molzen-Corbin is all about," says Archuleta.

2701 Miles Road SE, Albuquerque, NM 87106, 242-5700

Molzen-Corbin & Associates has provided engineering design at the Albuquerque International Sunport for over 30 years. At Sunport Boulevard (left photo) Kent S. Freier, senior civil engineer, and Joe P. Moore, chief civil engineer; and (right photo) on the airfield with Albuquerque's Director of Aviation Jay Czar and Mike Provine, senior airport engineer.

the Spirit of
URS CORPORATION, INC. est. 1961

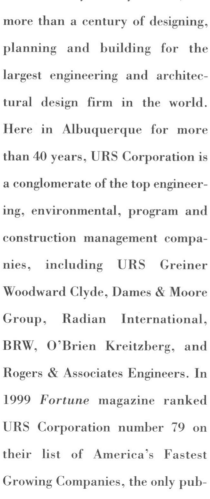

▶

Keeping our environment clean is an important part of URS Corporation's professional services.

232

Drive around Albuquerque and take a look at what URS Corporation is doing to improve the face of this city. Travel the "Big I" interchange and see how their state-of-the-art planning and design keeps traffic flowing. Cross the bridge over the Embudo Arroyo, a URS water resources management project. Visit Albuquerque International Sunport and enjoy the improvements that keep it one of the friendliest airports in the USA.

Everywhere you look, URS is making New Mexico move. These high-profile projects are the culmination of more than a century of designing, planning and building for the largest engineering and architectural design firm in the world. Here in Albuquerque for more than 40 years, URS Corporation is a conglomerate of the top engineering, environmental, program and construction management companies, including URS Greiner Woodward Clyde, Dames & Moore Group, Radian International, BRW, O'Brien Kreitzberg, and Rogers & Associates Engineers. In 1999 *Fortune* magazine ranked URS Corporation number 79 on their list of America's Fastest Growing Companies, the only publicly-owned engineering firm on that list. URS Corporation ranked number one in Pure Design for the second year in a row on the *Engineering News-Record*'s Top 500 Design Firms list in 1999. The firm is proud of its unmatched ability to provide specialized services in a myriad of markets. Whether the project is a new rail line or the remediation of a former military base, URS has and will rise to the challenge with the most sophisticated and comprehensive design and implementation capabilities in New Mexico and the world.

URS Corporation's roster of services includes expertise in the following fields: • Total transportation capabilities from worldwide leaders in surface, marine and air transportation • Engineering excellence in geotechnical and earth sciences, with specialties in soils and foundation engineering, field surveying and water resource solutions • Environmental planning to improve air and water quality, mitigate soil contamination and erosion, and manage hazardous waste • Collaborative resources that have effected solutions for multinational clients in the chemical, forest products, mining, oil and gas, aerospace and high-tech manufacturing

industries, among others • World-class facilities design, from corporate, health-care and educational complexes to stadiums and multi-use centers • Premier program/construction management services to deliver completed projects, on time and cost-effectively, anywhere in the world.

A local company with a multinational reputation, URS Corporation employs 125 people in New Mexico, most of them right here in Albuquerque. The company keeps the local community informed and involved in large construction projects that might temporarily alter daily activities in and around neighborhoods. URS honors and accommodates public input and opinion by keeping disruption to a minimum. For example, the Big I project information center is open to answer questions from residents, commuters and business owners who may be affected during the project. The well-being of Albuquerque's citizens is important to URS Corporation – after all, they live here, too.

From design/build projects to water resource management, from bike trails to the Big I, URS Corporation keeps Albuquerque on the go.

5971 Jefferson Boulevard NE, Suite 101, Albuquerque, NM 87109, 345-3999, www.urscorp.com

Albuquerque's US Postal Service Distribution Center, designed by URS, keeps New Mexico's communications moving.

2 3 3

URS plays a major design role in state-of-the-art transportation projects in Albuquerque (e.g., the Albuquerque International Sunport and the Big I).

With a strong national presence of over 6,000 branches in 21 states, Wells Fargo still has a long historical connection with and deep commitment to New Mexico. From its brightly lit building in downtown Albuquerque to its popular Miss Penny and Li'l Buck hot air balloons, Wells Fargo has left its mark on the state, and has shown its support of the Albuquerque community through both its philanthropy and financial services.

▶ Wells Fargo's new hot-air balloon, "A Loan at Last."

Tracing its roots in the West back to 1852, and in New Mexico back to 1962, the bank has a long-lived reputation for client loyalty and satisfaction. In November 1998, Wells Fargo merged with Norwest Bank New Mexico, making it the largest bank in the state and allowing an expansion of services to its customers at over 100 locations statewide.

In addition to traditional banking services such as loans and deposits, Wells Fargo is the largest provider of home mortgage loans in the United States, and their finance company has locations in all 50 states and the 10 provinces of Canada. It also offers its customers many convenient banking options, including phone banking, direct mail, grocery store loca-

Larry D. Willard, Chairman & CEO of Wells Fargo Bank New Mexico/ West Texas, displays a replica of a Wells Fargo stagecoach hand-crafted by a local bank customer.

tions, traditional bank stores and Internet banking. In fact, Wells Fargo is the current leader in Internet banking nationally.

Being the largest bank in the state has also put Wells Fargo in a position to fuel growth and prosperity in communities and businesses across the state. The bank has an array of business services that are offered to companies of all sizes, including large corporate financing, real estate lending, business lines of credit and cash management services.

The bank also prides itself on being on the leading edge of technology in the financial services industry. Thanks to new technology, examples of new services include such innovations as allowing individual customers to have overdrafts to their deposit accounts charged to their Visa or MasterCard credit cards, which saves on overdraft fees. In addition, small companies can now have excess funds swept out of their deposit account and invested in mutual funds on a nightly basis.

Wells Fargo's commitment to New Mexico spans beyond its array of financial services. It also gives back to the community in a number of ways. In Albuquerque alone, the bank supports a number of charities, including the Explora Science Center and Children's Museum of Albuquerque, the National Hispanic Cultural Center, Albuquerque Public Schools, the University of New Mexico and the Albuquerque Community Foundation. The bank is also very committed to and involved in civic organizations, such as the Greater Albuquerque Chamber of Commerce, the Hispano Chamber of Commerce, the Economic Forum, Albuquerque Economic Development and the Downtown Action Team.

And then, of course, there are the hot-air balloons! Wells Fargo's "A Loan At Last," "High Yield," "Miss Penny" and "Li'l Buck" balloons are so well known by

Wells Fargo has fueled growth and prosperity in businesses and communities statewide.

residents that they have become an integral part of Albuquerque's public image and the Kodak Albuquerque International Balloon Fiesta®, where the bank is the sponsor of the Special Shapes Rodeo®. In fact, when the banks merged in 1998, the primary question among Albuquerqueans was not so much how bank services would change, but rather whether the bank would continue to keep its beloved hot-air balloons.

With the bank's strong dedication to the people of New Mexico, those clients need not worry. Wells Fargo is here to stay...still local, still committed to our communities.

200 Lomas Boulevard NW, Albuquerque, NM 87102, (800) 396-BANK (2265), www.wellsfargo.com

Wells Fargo's new lighting system lights up the downtown area, displaying the spirit of Albuquerque.

Mechanical systems are invisible. Customer relationships are not. New Mexico's largest mechanical and engineering contractor knows that, in their business, reputations rest on the bedrock of client relationships nurtured and maintained over years of success. Yearout Mechanical & Engineering takes pride in the connections they've made with clients over nearly 40 years in business.

▶ Yearout's design/build approach to mechanical engineering brings a project from drawing board to finished product.

Trust keeps customers coming back to Yearout Mechanical & Engineering, Inc. – trust in their design/build capabilities, trust in Yearout's ability to stay on track with time and costs, and implicit trust in their professionalism and standards of safety. Their clients are a roster of Who's Who in New Mexico – Intel, Philips Semiconductor, Sandia National Laboratory, Presbyterian Healthcare,

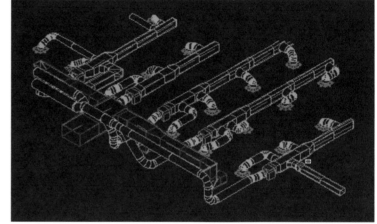

Klinger Construction, Sumitomo SITIX Silicon, and many other tough customers who return to Yearout again and again for their mechanical and engineering needs. In fact, all of Yearout's customers are repeat customers.

Design/build and fast-track construction have made Yearout a standout in the mechanical and engineering field.

Partnership and trust are vital elements of Yearout's customer relationships.

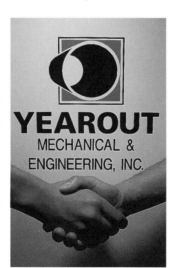

"So often, customers say to us, 'Do what you think is best,'" says President Kevin Yearout. "We can make a sketch to fit a client's verbal specifications, then work with architects and general contractors to build it. Creativity can be a rare quality. Our staff has tons of it." The firm takes pride, too, in their fast turnaround of design/build projects for clients as diverse as high-technology companies, light manufacturing companies and hospitals.

Founded in 1963 by CEO Kim Yearout and his father, Robert, Yearout Mechanical & Engineering has grown to 250 employees. This third-generation, family-owned business also employs families who have worked there for two and three generations—fathers and sons, fathers and daughters, husbands and wives. Kevin Yearout is convinced that employee loyalty is one of his company's most important assets. "We rely on them to produce quality work and keep us up and running," he says, adding, "and they must feel the same way. We put a lot into our people, in training and ongoing education. We have an extraordinarily low turnover for the construction industry in general." Kevin's brother, Bryan Yearout, is vice president and Lian Yearout, Kevin's wife, is the company controller.

YEAROUT
MECHANICAL &
ENGINEERING, INC.

Yearout's most important training program concerns safety. Nationally, they ranked first, second and first in safety in 1997, 1998 and 1999, according to Sheet Metal and Air Conditioning Contractors National Association (SMACNA). "We work really hard at it," says Kevin Yearout. "Our employees act as our safety committee. They believe that any injury can be prevented." In addition, the company's quality-conscious procedures recently garnered Yearout a Roadrunner Award from Quality New Mexico.

Yearout Mechanical & Engineering recognizes the contributions of their founder, Kim Yearout, to their industry. Nationally and locally, Kim serves on the boards of professional organizations and labor committees. Yearout's employees follow Kim's lead: they donate their time and expertise to a long list of community fundraisers for charity and sit on the boards of many local organizations. The Yearout family, and all of its families, are happy to be a vital part of Albuquerque's residential and business communities. **3228 Los Arboles Road NE, Albuquerque, NM 87107, 884-0994, www.yearout.com**

Clients return again and again to Yearout for their mechanical and engineering needs.

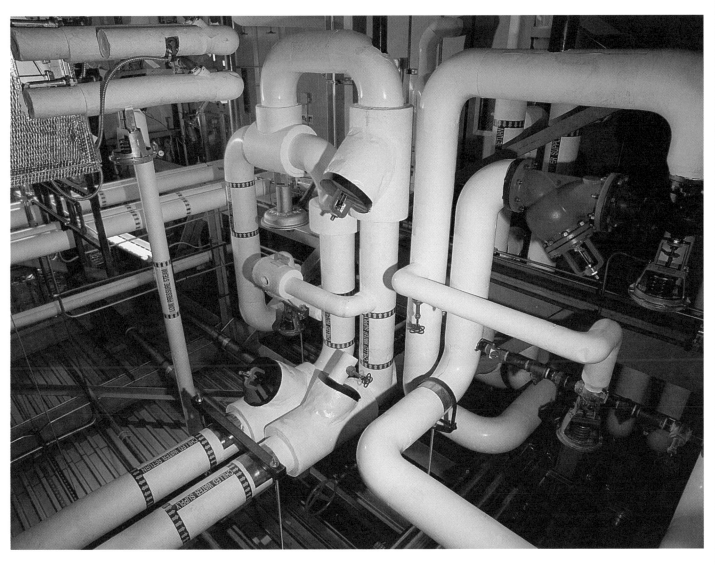

Yearout projects appear in locations throughout the city: high-technology companies, light manufacturing companies and hospitals.

237

the spirit of
THE BRANCH LAW FIRM est. 1966

Protecting the citizens of New Mexico – and the world – from environmental hazards and physical harm is the Branch Law Firm's most important and dearest mission. Since it was founded in 1966, the firm has dedicated itself to supporting people's rights through its expertise in civil jury trials and complex civil and mass tort litigation. The firm has

shown its dedication to the community by winning or settling dozens of cases and not letting environmental polluters and careless manufacturers off the hook. The firm is heavily involved in complex litigation, including class actions and multi-district civil cases, cases consolidated for trial, as well as products liability, personal injury, medical malpractice, aviation and railroad cases.

▶ Turner and Margaret Branch at their offices located in the historic Rio Grande Corridor.

The firm recently was retained by the New Mexico Attorney General to pursue Superfund Toxic Tort Cleanup cases in the state, and recently represented the State of New Mexico against the big tobacco companies, which resulted in a $1.2 billion settlement for the State. The Branch Law Firm has also been involved in the breast implant litigation, Norplant contraceptive litigation, L-Tryptophan litigation, and is currently involved in the Fen-Phen litigation. In these cases, the firm continues to fight to protect the rights of thousands of New Mexicans.

The firm also has a long history with—and deep commitment to—New Mexico. It was founded by Turner W. Branch, a University of New Mexico graduate, in 1966, and Branch was joined by his wife, Margaret Moses Branch, a fourth-generation New Mexican, in 1978.

The Branch family has shown its dedication to New Mexico through serving on many public boards and assisting many local charities. They have donated time and money to St. John's Episcopal Cathedral, the University of New Mexico Law School and the University of New Mexico Foundation Board. In addition, Turner W. Branch was a member of the State Legislature from 1968 to 1974, and Rebecca Claire Branch, Turner's daughter and an associate in the firm, is currently the attorney for the Village of Los Ranchos. Mr. Branch has also served on the Board of Directors for the Better Business Bureau and the Albuquerque Little Theater.

238

Over the years the firm has continued to spread out across the country. It currently has offices in Houston, Texas; Durango, Colorado; and Albuquerque, New Mexico, where it was founded. But the Branch firm also realizes the importance and quality of being in New Mexico, a state it has deep roots in. "Albuquerque provides a small-town atmosphere with the opportunities of a growing city," Turner W. Branch says. "I feel we couldn't have had the same growth pattern as a law firm in most cities in the U.S.

The firm has a long history with — and deep commitment to — New Mexico.

Albuquerque was an opportunity for us – and we were able to fit into the community and be in the right place at the right time. We've grown with the city and I think it's a very special place for us to be."

2025 Rio Grande Boulevard NW, Albuquerque, NM 87104, 243-3500, www.branchlawfirm.com

Everyone at the Branch Law Firm works hard to protect the rights of their fellow Americans and New Mexicans.

the Spirit of
OCTOPUS CAR WASH est. 1968

240

Full-service car washing just hasn't been the same since John Jurkens opened the first Octopus Car Wash in 1953. The high-tech, low-touch systems of Octopus Car Wash upped the standards in the car wash industry, forever raising customer expectations of a scratchless, brush-free experience. Octopus even uses soap manufactured by their own company, environmentally friendly and so gentle you can wash your face in it. Along with water pressure that loosens and removes the dirt buildup on your vehicle's surface, their special ph-balanced soap gives your car a no-friction shampoo. Octopus Car Wash took a giant step for the car wash industry when they invented this special wash process.

The folks at Octopus Car Wash know that you want to get a great car wash, fast and at a reasonable price. They get you in and out in no time at all, with the best products and service around. Their wash process includes vacuuming, cleaning of interior and exterior windows, and complete, speedy towel drying of your vehicle's exterior. Octopus Car Wash provides an assortment of additional services such as spray waxing, mat and wheel cleaning, Armorall treatment, paste waxing and carpet shampooing.

If you have a little more time, additional services include interior cleaning of seats and carpets, which can take up to 40 minutes, and for those in a hurry, we offer express hand waxing. Hand waxing may take as little as 5 minutes and rarely takes more than 20 minutes. These waxes are designed to help protect your vehicle from harmful environmental exposure while providing your vehicle with a protective shine.

The paste waxes that Octopus uses are specially designed to clean the vehicle of oxidation and soils while providing a protective shield. They use an orbital buffer to enhance the benefit of the wax. These waxes will restore the luster to almost any vehicle's paint. Octopus recommends that customers have their vehicles waxed regularly to prevent any oxidation from occurring. This waxing process takes approximately 40 minutes.

Son-in-law (front), father, son (rear).

Octopus Car Wash came to Albuquerque in 1969 and has four locations throughout the city; there have been as many as 33 locations throughout the country. You can't miss them: Ozzie the Octopus sits atop each one, overseeing operations. Octopus Car Wash is a family-owned, second-generation business founded by John Jurkens and operated by him, his two sons and his two daughters, all of whom grew up in this business and love it. On any given day, you might find a member of the family working on your car at any one of their four locations. That's the kind of commitment Octopus makes to their customers, that they'll always see things from your side.

As "Ozzie" the Octopus always says, "A clean car rides better and lasts longer."

Octopus Car Wash is dedicated to making and keeping happy customers. Their super services extend the life and retain the quality of your vehicle. Your resale value will be far greater when it is time to trade up; of course, your old car might look so good you won't want a new one.

As "Ozzie" the Octopus always says, "A clean car rides better and lasts longer."

Four locations in the Albuquerque area, www.octopuscarwash.com

From left:
father John,
son-in-law Charlie,
son Joel,
daughter Jill.

241

SAIC's shareholders have a real stake in the company's success. That's because 95 percent of the company's 38,000 employees own SAIC stock. Does this cutting-edge brand of employee compensation drive SAIC's people to excellence? Several hundred of their employees are millionaires. You do the math.

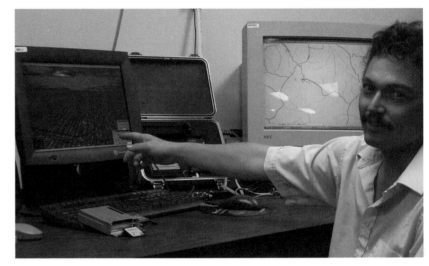

J. Robert Beyster, a physicist formerly of Los Alamos National Laboratory, founded the company in 1969, with two government contracts for nuclear power and weapons research. SAIC analyzed data from the reactor at Three-Mile Island following the nuclear accident there in 1980. In 1987 the company acquired AMSEC, a $20 million provider of ship engineering and maintenance services to the U.S. Navy. SAIC bought Network Solutions in 1995, the exclusive registrar for Internet domain names like .com and .org. They formed a joint venture with the world's second-largest oil producer, Petroleos de Venezuela (PDVSA), in 1996, to provide information technology services to that company. Recently, SAIC acquired Bellcore, the 5,000-employee-strong research arm of the Bell companies operating in the Northeastern United States.

Dr. Beyster believes in sharing company performance and profit directly with employees. "We believe that those who help the company grow should own it, and that ownership should be commensurate with that contribution and performance as much as is feasible," he says. In 1974 Beyster formed a registered broker-dealer, Bull, Inc., to handle all SAIC employee trades. SAIC's stock is evaluated quarterly, using a formula based on the company's net income and the stock values of publicly traded competitors like Computer Sciences and EDS. SAIC's employee-owner relations division handles inquiries from employee shareholders. Dr. Beyster believes so strongly in tying employee incentives to corporate performance that in 1986, he endowed the Foundation for Enterprise Development to promote his own philosophy of employee ownership.

SAIC is the largest employee-owned research and engineering firm in the United States, and in April 1999 they were ranked number 347 among the Fortune 500 companies. Their Test and Evaluation Group is headquartered in

Albuquerque, with 450 employee-owners working on projects as diverse as flight and performance simulation, environmental impact assessment, and medical database processing for government, military and private-sector clients. SAIC's high-tech capabilities, for example, serve the Department of Defense and Kirtland Air Force Base in modeling and simulation, field test support and instrumentation. Their experienced, hands-on planning, execution, data management, analysis and reporting have supported technological demonstrations of future-generation air vehicles and ground-based weapons systems. For private busi-

SAIC brings work of global importance to the city of Albuquerque.

ness, SAIC develops secure payment protocols over the Internet, and provides innovative telecommunications solutions. SAIC's problem-solving abilities begin with access to any technology, for any customer, anywhere in the world.

SAIC brings work of global importance to the city of Albuquerque. Responsive to technological changes in business and the world, they provide solutions to the problems of governments, industries and communities. Their employee-owners and senior leaders participate in important civic associations like the Greater Albuquerque Chamber of Commerce, and in financial and economic forums about the future of the region. In fact, with their local commitments, global expertise and unique way of attracting and motivating entrepreneurial employees, SAIC is inventing the future.

6200 Uptown Boulevard NE, Suite 300, Albuquerque, NM 87110, 837-2976

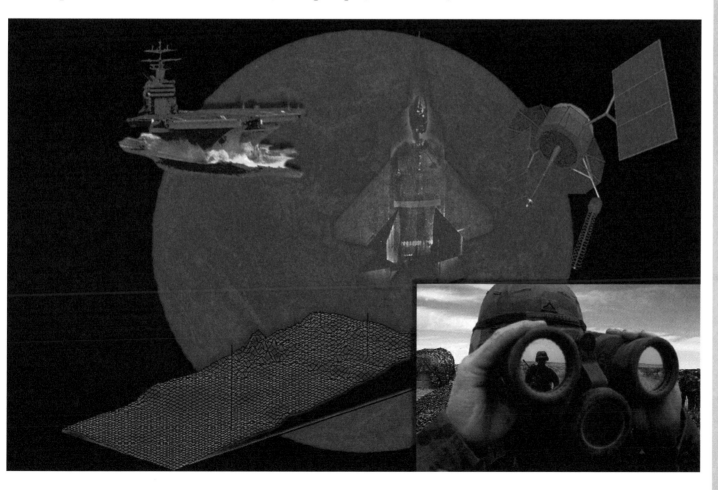

the spirit of
CB RICHARD ELLIS est. 1974

2 4 4

CB Richard Ellis may be a huge commercial real estate firm with 10,000 employees in over 230 offices in more than 30 countries, but it believes in Albuquerque. You don't find many international companies in a city the size of Albuquerque, but CB Richard Ellis thinks Albuquerque's unique combination of high-tech and traditional businesses, cultural attractions and enchantment are a perfect match for the company's flair and skill in the real estate market.

"The fact that we're in Albuquerque speaks well for the city and its future. There are plenty of cities our size where CBRE doesn't have a presence," says Steve Monroe, Managing Director of the Albuquerque office. "But we believe this is a city of the future, and we want to be here to grow as we help the city grow."

CB Richard Ellis can trace part of its history back to England in 1773, when Richard Ellis first established his REI Ltd. firm in London. In the 1960s, REI Ltd. expanded to become a worldwide expert in property investment and corporate advice. Then, in 1998, REI Ltd. merged with CB Commercial, a national company that also had a long history in commercial real estate, being founded in 1906 in San Francisco. Once together as CB Richard Ellis, the company took the forefront in its field, offering the industry's most comprehensive portfolio of services in offices around the world. These core services include property sales and leasing, property management, corporate advisory services, facilities management, mortgage banking, investment management, capital markets, appraisal/valuation, research and consulting.

The company's presence in Albuquerque began in 1974, when it received an assignment to handle the leasing of the Coronado Mall. A permanent office was started in 1983, which today boasts the most experienced brokerage, property management and research staff in Albuquerque. CB Richard Ellis' Albuquerque staff focuses on six commercial real estate areas – office space, retail, industrial, land, investment properties and apartments. The company's sales professionals specialize in only one of those areas, which helps them focus their energy and be more competent at meeting their clients' specific needs.

"We try to remain pure to those specialties so that we're the best in town in that particular area," Monroe says. "If we focus on just one specialty, we can know it best, and we can be known for knowing it the best. I believe that this focused approach is unique in this marketplace, and it's an ingrained part of our corporate culture."

The company is well known around the world by owners, investors and occupiers alike for its consistency in service and professionalism. In fact, being part of the CB Richard Ellis family makes Albuquerque a notable part of the global real estate environment.

"I've met people from Milan, Perth and Zimbabwe, all of whom have the same business card we have," Monroe says. "To be in Albuquerque and to have that feeling of how

> We believe Albuquerque is a city of the future, and we want to grow as we help the city grow.

small the world is and how much we as a company and a city are part of that bigger world is really exciting."

The Albuquerque office of CB Richard Ellis (NYSE:CBG) is located at:
Two Park Square, 6565 Americas Parkway NE, Suite 110, Albuquerque, New Mexico 87110, 837-4999, www.cbrichardellis.com

Our Albuquerque staff of experienced professionals provide access to the unparalleled menu of services offered by CB Richard Ellis worldwide.

the **spirit** of

ALBUQUERQUE HISPANO CHAMBER OF COMMERCE est. 1975

As one of the oldest and most reputable Hispanic organizations in the country, the Albuquerque Hispano Chamber of Commerce is making sure Albuquerque's rainbow of businesses thrive. Since it was founded in 1975, the organization has aggressively pursued new projects and opportunities to enhance Albuquerque's businesses and draws more than $20 million into the city every year.

▶
Traditional flamenco dancers are part of modern Hispanic culture.

The Albuquerque Hispano chamber promotes tourism and brings conferences and new businesses to Albuquerque, but it also has a larger role in developing the city's economy and work force. The chamber is working on a number of hands-on projects heading into the new millennium, including building the Barelas Job Opportunity Center, which will house the chamber, a Job Opportunity Center and provide approximately 3,000 square feet of space for commercial and retail businesses. The Job Opportunity Center will provide computer training, and business and life-skills classes to enhance the development of the city's work force. It will also function as a natural conduit into TVI's Workforce Training Center, where employers can work with potential employees to further enhance New Mexico's work force.

The chamber also places a strong emphasis on students through its school-to-work program, which serves as a model for similar programs across the nation. "School-to-work is very important," says Loretta Armenta, President and CEO of the Albuquerque Hispano Chamber of Commerce. "Young people need to get real life experiences before they get out of school and go on to college

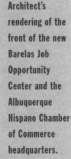

Architect's rendering of the front of the new Barelas Job Opportunity Center and the Albuquerque Hispano Chamber of Commerce headquarters.

and into the workplace, and we need to provide them with that opportunity." In addition, the chamber donates $50,000 in scholarships every year to deserving young people.

Another Albuquerque Hispano chamber goal is to help businesses move into the future by learning about e-commerce and the Internet. The chamber provides a number of classes to help business people learn hands-on about new technology. The chamber has always provided a

number of valuable services to the business community, including help with strategic planning, tax and legal problems and marketing development.

The not-for-profit Albuquerque Hispano Chamber of Commerce is funded through membership, federal and state school-to-work grants, contracts with the city of Albuquerque and the city's lodgers tax.

The chamber's mission is to improve the quality of life in the Hispanic community by promoting economic and educational opportunities with an emphasis on small business.

Historically the Albuquerque Hispano chamber has always welcomed and encouraged diversity within the organization. "We want to make a difference, to have an impact – not just in terms of helping to build small business-es, but also to encourage the spirit of entrepreneurship among all people," Armenta says.

"We want to make our community better. Our goal is to see that it secures an economically sound foundation and is a safe environment for every one who lives in it."

202 Central Avenue SE, Suite 300, Albuquerque, NM 87102, 842-9003, www.ahcnm.org

Local Hispanic culture and business goes back hundreds of years, to the founding of Albuquerque's Old Town Plaza and San Felipe de Neri church.

the Spirit of
ALBUQUERQUE CONVENTION & VISITORS BUREAU est. 1980

Drawing tourists and conventions can help a community's economy thrive and flourish, and that's just what the Albuquerque Convention and Visitors Bureau (ACVB) does for Albuquerque. Founded in 1980, the not-for profit ACVB has provided outreach, assisted in planning and encouraged leisure travelers and meeting planners to visit and hold conventions in this historic and charming city.

The ACVB is supported by lodgers tax and private revenue from members and other sources. Through its membership, the ACVB brings the wide array of Albuquerque businesses – including hotels, restaurants, tourist attractions and local transportation companies – to tourists and meeting planners. ACVB supplies information services to assist tourists on everything the city offers. It supports four Visitor Information Centers and phone hotlines.

The ACVB promotes the city through regional and national marketing efforts with a focus on Albuquerque's celebrated reputation as a dynamic metropolis, filled with the magic of living history, cutting-edge technology, multiculturalism, natural beauty, a thriving arts community and a deep commitment to quality of life. In all of this, it further promotes Albuquerque as a desirable meeting and convention destination nationwide.

The ACVB is involved in supporting the Kodak Albuquerque International Balloon Fiesta, the most popular ballooning event in the world, as well as many other attractions and events in and around Albuquerque, giving the visitor an opportunity for vast cultural, scenic and scientific experiences.

Attractions in the diverse city of Albuquerque include Historic Old Town, the location of the original Spanish villa from which Albuquerque grew; Petroglyph National Monument, featuring an estimated 17,000 rock etchings carved over thousands of years; Sandia Peak Tramway, the world's largest continuous single-span aerial tramway, which climbs to 10,378 feet; and the Indian Pueblo Cultural Center, where visitors can experience the art, history and culture of the region's 19 American Indian Pueblos

Historic Old Town is a favorite for Albuquerque visitors, providing a unique shopping experience.

The ACVB Visitor Information Centers provide a variety of free, friendly information and brochures to visitors.

2
4
8

Supporting and encouraging tourists to visit the city is vital to its economic well-being. Tourism currently provides over 48,000 jobs in New Mexico and is currently the state's second-largest industry, producing $3.394 billion in revenues. In Albuquerque alone, 3.2 million visitors generate $1.35 billion in revenues.

The money tourists spend in Albuquerque helps the community to thrive and grow by providing jobs, helping local businesses, and by affecting almost every area of the economy, including hotels, transportation, restaurants and retail. Those dollars also support local infrastructure such as downtown revitalization, promoting the arts, expanding sports and entertainment events and facilities, preserving historical attractions and creating cultural events and attractions.

> Supporting and encouraging tourists to visit the city is vital to its economic well-being.

ACVB represents over 1,000 companies and organizations in the city and is a vital resource for the economic growth of this beautiful region. In addition, it aids and enhances tourists' enjoyment of this historic, culturally diverse and attraction-filled place we call the Land of Enchantment.

20 First Plaza NW, Suite 601, Albuquerque, NM 87102, 842-9918, 800-733-9918, www.abqcvb.org

Albuquerque offers visitors a unique blend of history, adventure, culture, arts and technology.

the Spirit of
VAUGHN WEDEEN CREATIVE, INC. est. 1982

Uncharted territory is frightening, exhilarating, fresh, wild. New Mexico once seemed that way to two New Yorkers and a Texan who moved here for the blue skies and mapped their own roads to bliss. Twenty years later, Rick Vaughn and Steve Wedeen and Richard Kuhn still feel inspired by the beauty of their chosen home. The combined portfolio of Vaughn Wedeen Creative answers the grandeur of this place with a visual landscape as imaginative, colorful and one-of-a-kind as an Albuquerque sunset.

▶ This was our treat to the Albuquerque Zoo to help them scare up some funds on Halloween.

Vaughn Wedeen Creative is a creative consultancy and design group that pushes the possibilities of image and ideas. From a modest start in 1982, the firm zoomed into the wild blue to become an internationally-known company, garnering hundreds of awards along the way for their corporate identity programs, print ads, posters, brochures and packaging. Their clients are leading players on a global stage in telecommunications, tourism, construction, civic matters and the arts. For them, Vaughn Wedeen wraps corporate initiatives in images that can convey the importance of a policy or product, the urgency of a new discovery, or the reason for a company's entire existence. The creative staff at Vaughn Wedeen doesn't believe in canned answers to the directive, "Show me the path to success." Vaughn Wedeen writes new rules to uniquely express a company's character, quality and vision. Think of them as experienced, creative guides through the world of change that defines corporate communications today.

Talk about space. Colorful and whimsical. Vaughn Wedeen's environment is as playful as it is practical. An experience as exciting as it is efficient. And one that begins as soon as you enter the door.

Drop by Vaughn Wedeen and see how good design communicates and entertains. At their offices in the Old Town section of Albuquerque, the company has outgrown their original first floor space to occupy most of the building they now co-own. Wit and whimsy rule. Columns swirl, colors entice, there are walls without boundaries. The immediate impact hits you like Vaughn

Wedeen's client designs – this is different, distinctive. They know their audience. They *are* their audience.

Vaughn Wedeen's clients include Fortune 500 companies such as Time Warner, U S West, Motorola and AT&T, as well as several prominent New Mexico corporations. The firm shows its deep commitment to promoting the arts in New Mexico with pro bono and reduced-rate work for many community and arts organizations. From the Albuquerque Plaza to the Duke City marathon, the Santa Fe Opera to the Rio Grande Zoo, everywhere you look, Vaughn Wedeen has created original ways to make people sit up and take notice.

We live in a highly sophisticated visual environment. Image often speaks louder than words.

Most people don't get to practice their passion every day. At Vaughn Wedeen Creative, they love their work. And that pioneering passion works for their clients.

407 Rio Grande Boulevard NW, Albuquerque, NM 87104, 243-4000, www.vwc.com

Our study guide played well for Pecos River Learning Center's self-empowerment team-building course.

the Spirit of
NEW MEXICO TECHNET est. 1984

Through its dedication to state-of-the-art technology and its commitment to quality service, New Mexico Technet is helping New Mexico stay on top and thrive in today's ever-expanding high-tech Internet and e-commerce marketplace. Established in 1984 as a private non-profit organization, Technet was the first Internet service provider in New Mexico, and the company continues to expand its vast array of services, providing a vital resource to individuals and businesses throughout the state.

▶ Technet: Internet access for business.

"We want to be considered the Internet service company in New Mexico that provides multiple options to fill the needs of businesses in their day-to-day operations," says Marlin D. Coffee, President and CEO of Technet. "We also want to connect New Mexico's rural communities in a way that places them on a level playing field with the more densely populated cities in this state."

Approximately 80 percent of commercial Internet traffic in New Mexico flows through New Mexico

Technet offers the widest range of Internet services available. From dedicated access, like DSL and DDS, to the web and e-commerce, Technet leads the way.

Technet and its for-profit subsidiary, Oso Grande Technologies, Inc. The company is well known for its steadfast reliability and quality of service.

Throughout its history, Technet has dedicated itself to its progressive mission of providing New Mexicans access to the Internet for all the potential it has to offer. It has provided free connections to schools and teachers and has fostered the development of high-tech on-line services to the state's growing economic sector.

"We have a commitment to our state and the communities that we serve," Coffee says. "We believe in the furtherance of the educational process and other non-profit activities that will provide a level of culture and educational opportunities for the citizens of this state."

Thanks to Technet, 98 percent of the population of New Mexico can now take advantage of on-line services provided by the company and other Internet service providers who rely on Technet for their Internet services. And that's what Technet is all about — keeping New Mexico competitive and healthy, on technology's cutting edge.

5921 Jefferson Boulevard NE, Suite A, Albuquerque, NM 87109, 345-6555, www.technet.nm.org

That's what Technet is all about — keeping New Mexico on technology's cutting edge.

Marlin Coffee, president, enjoys a quiet moment in Technet's state-of-the-art training facility.

255

the Spirit of
STARLIGHT PUBLISHING est. 1985

Keeping New Mexico informed and healthy is the concept that drives Starlight Publishing. The company helps the state's communities grow by publishing a wide variety of visitor, relocation and economic development guides, drawing outside interest to the state's many wonders. Starlight also helps keep New Mexicans informed and in touch with the business scene, by publishing *New Mexico Business Weekly.*

"It is important to all of us at Starlight that we play a very vital role in the community," says Rick Homans, Starlight's Chairman and CEO. "That's what makes our work so worthwhile – the knowledge that we make a difference."

Starlight Publishing, in a lot of ways, mirrors the growth of Albuquerque. As the community has grown, prospered and developed so has this company."

Since its founding in 1985, the company has truly grown with the communities of New Mexico, transforming itself from a small one-magazine company into a large creative and entrepreneurial entity that produces more than 15 magazines and newspapers, including *Absolutely Albuquerque,* the *Albuquerque Visitors Guide,* the *Official Santa Fe Visitors Guide, Indian Market Magazine,* and the *Farmington Area Guide.*

New Mexico Business Weekly, one of Starlight's crowning achievements, also has thrived and grown along with the state's business community. Founded in 1994, the paper is a vital resource to the state's businesses, keeping them up to date on key news and information. Along with its weekly coverage, the newspaper staff also publishes a quarterly Commercial Real Estate supplement, the quarterly *Wells Fargo New Mexico Market Report,* the *Book of Business Lists and Power Brokers,* the *How-To Guide,* and the *Annual Report.*

"Our goal at the *Business Weekly* is to initiate dialogue and lead discussions of the very complex issues facing our state, such as growth and development, and education reform," Homans says. "There's a leadership vacuum when it comes to New Mexico media; *New Mexico Business Weekly* has already begun to play an active role in filling that void. We will continue to grow the newspaper as a powerful media and business tool."

Keeping New Mexicans informed and in touch with the business scene: New Mexico Business Weekly.

Rick Homans, Starlight Publishing's Chairman and CEO, has led the company since 1988.

2
5
4

On the contract publishing side, Starlight has worked with a number of communities, including Albuquerque, Rio Rancho, Santa Fe, Farmington and Gallup – to publish visitor guides and other recruitment tools used to draw business and tourism into the state. "We pride ourselves on being able to create from scratch world-class marketing tools for New Mexico's communities and businesses," Homans says. "We take the job from concept to creation to delivery."

Over the years, the company has also shown a strong dedication to community service. Homans has served on the board of directors of the Greater Albuquerque Chamber of Commerce, Albuquerque Convention and Visitors Bureau, Albuquerque Community Foundation and La Compania de Teatro de Alburquerque. And other Starlight employees are continually involved in a host of other civic organizations, lending their time, creative talents and organizational skills to causes locally and statewide.

> "The health of our business depends on the health of the community. We help out however we can."

"The health of our business depends completely on the health of the community," Homans says. "So we roll up our sleeves and help out however we can."

625 Silver SW, Albuquerque, NM 87102, 768-7008, www.nmbw.nmsource.com, www.starlightpub.com

World-class marketing tools for New Mexico's communities are a source of pride for both Starlight and the organizations so beautifully and effectively represented.

the Spirit of
BGK PROPERTIES est. 1992

In 1992 a group of investors formed BGK Properties, headquartered in Santa Fe. Since that time BGK has grown substantially and currently owns 18 million square feet nationwide, in 25 states, with over 2 million square feet of that total located in Albuquerque. An asset to New Mexico, BGK is financially sound and has national stature as a major real estate owner and manager.

▶ Pinetree Corporate Center, a centrally located office park off of I-40 in Albuquerque.

In addition to its financial stability, the diverse experience of BGK's senior management is one of the company's strengths. The founders of BGK came to real estate from the worlds of investment and financial services, law, commercial lending and high technology. Attracted by the lifestyle and beauty of New Mexico, most of the senior management were new to the state in the early '90s and brought with them years of experience in their respective businesses on the East and West Coasts. When the U.S. real estate market fell on hard

"The Citadel," a Class A building in uptown Albuquerque.

times in the late 1980s and 1990s, the founders saw an opportunity to acquire excellent properties for 30 to 50 percent of their then-replacement cost. Such opportunities rarely occur, and BGK was positioned to take full advantage of the situation.

BGK believes tenant-friendly management enhances the value of each commercial property. Their hands-on style keeps BGK's corporate asset managers in touch with their property managers nationwide and directly involved in the management of those properties every day. In areas in which BGK has a high concentration of buildings, the company establishes its own management firm. BGK employs 30 people in Albuquerque and outsources the leasing of its properties to third-party companies in Albuquerque. In Santa Fe, BGK employs 60 people at its headquarters. This privately-held company also owns properties in Santa Fe, Hobbs and Las Cruces.

Real estate owners, agents and managers are prominent movers and shakers in any city. They bring considerable expertise to commercial site selection and property development and help create opportunities to bring new business into town. BGK's investment in Albuquerque is a ringing endorsement of the city's burgeoning economic powers and its attraction for people and companies outside the state. With office space, industrial and retail holdings, BGK keeps many different types of commercial tenants happy, citywide. BGK is able to provide any business contemplating a move to Albuquerque with a wide variety of buildings to satisfy their space needs. From Uptown to the Renaissance area, the Northeast Heights to the West Mesa, BGK has the city covered with quality commercial buildings for lease, a significant presence that brings business to Albuquerque's table.

BGK's investment in Albuquerque is a ringing endorsement of the city's economic power.

330 Garfield Street, Santa Fe, NM 87501, 992-5100, www.bgkgroup.com

First Plaza in downtown Albuquerque, headquarters of BGK Asset Management.

EMCORE PhotoVoltaics (EPV) makes solar cells that convert light to electricity. A subsidiary of EMCORE Corporation, the world leader in fully integrated compound semiconductor solutions, EPV serves the global communications market by manufacturing these solar cells for use in the space industry. EPV solar cells are used in the telecommunications satellites sent into space by every major satellite manufacturing company in the world.

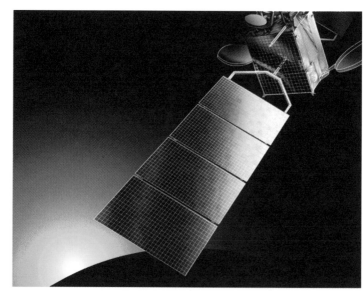

Solar cells provide power for satellites in space.

EPV's solar cells are advanced, sophisticated and highly efficient. They reduce the weight of satellite solar arrays by 50 percent, reduce the wing area and improve radiation tolerance. EPV's solar cells have a higher light-to-power conversion, which increases payload capacity and economic return. EPV's solar cells outperform every other solar cell made today. This use of efficient materials and design, along with a longer maintenance interval, lowers solar cell production costs, offering satellite manufacturers distinct advantages in a highly competitive marketplace.

High quality solar cell materials are grown in Emcore's own proven TurboDisc MOCVD platform chamber.

Situated in its own 50,000-square-foot building in Albuquerque, near Sandia National Laboratory, EPV is a new company with a unique manufacturing system. It is fully automated, making solar cells by means of machines and robots, resulting in more consistent processing, an overall better yield and a cleaner facility. Some of the robots are customized for EPV; others are standard models used in other types of manufacturing operations. Using EMCORE's own proven TurboDiscR MOCVD tools, EPV provides cost-effective solutions for solar cell manufacturing. They have the highest throughput in the industry, and the highest yield of epitaxial materials. All EPV production takes place in a Class 100-1000 clean room with state-of-the-art growth, processing and test equipment. This reliable manufacturing process produces exceptional material uniformity and reproducibility. It also helps EPV maintain its stated goal: to supply their customers with defect-free products and services that meet their requirements through continuous improvement of EPV's quality systems.

Some features of EPV's solar cells include: • Dual-Junction N on P polarity • Epitaxial materials grow in EMCORE's patented reactors with excellent uniformity and repeatability • Cells can be welded or soldered • Greater than three times the mechanical strength of other cells of its type • Optimized electrical performance • Mass savings: flat profile means ease of laydown and reduced adhesive • 20 percent more surface area for increased power.

Only three factories in the world manufacture solar cells for this application. Only one is in Albuquerque. EPV employs 100 people, 90 percent of whom are from New Mexico, many of whom have doctoral degrees. Many employees are graduates of the University of New Mexico, TVI and other institutions of higher learning. Whenever possible, EPV buys materials used in the manufacturing process locally. This rapidly growing company is part of an expanding industry that has already earned New Mexico a place in the high-technology lexicon and a global reputation as a place where forward-thinking industry can thrive. EMCORE PhotoVoltaics is pleased to be part of Albuquerque's exciting future.

10420 Research Road SE, Albuquerque, NM 87123, 332-5000, www.emcore.com

> EPV is part of an industry that has earned New Mexico a place in the high-technology lexicon.

Large numbers of four-inch diameter wafers are loaded in vacuum chambers for deposition of metals to make solar cells.

the Spirit of
STRONG-THORNE MORTUARY est. 1882

In the nineteenth century, furniture makers also made the occasional coffin. By 1882, O.W. and Henry Strong had expanded into funeral service to serve the community in what was to become downtown Albuquerque. Today, O.W.'s great-great granddaughter, Cezanne "Zizi" Terrasas, manages the facilities and carries on the family vocation with personalized, family-oriented services for all faiths.

When the Strong brothers' wagon broke down in Albuquerque in 1878, they didn't know they would become the founders of a five-generation tradition. From 1882 until today, Strong-Thorne Mortuary helps families commemorate the lives of their loved ones.

"Funeral services are for the living," Zizi says. "They should be tailored to the needs and wishes of each family." Strong-Thorne offers contemporary and traditional services, personally designed dedications that can be set in a chapel or in a forest. Families might even opt for a scattering of ashes from a space shuttle, a choice O.W. himself never contemplated. "We strive to help families remember their loved one in a way that is meaningful to them," Zizi notes.

Strong-Thorne offers other services to help families plan for a funeral, and to help them following a death. Bereavement support groups are conducted, along with sessions on helping children understand death. Speakers are available to talk to community groups about death, grief and funeral education. Strong-Thorne's doors are always open to anyone who might have questions about funeral services, cremation and the costs of these services.

In 1988 Strong-Thorne Mortuary became associated with Fitzgerald and Son Funeral Directors, Inc., a family-owned firm established by Robert Fitzgerald and Edward J. Fitzgerald in 1965. In 1988 Strong-Thorne and Fitzgerald and Son were privileged to be affiliated with the Loewen Group International, Inc., family of funeral homes. Together, they continue a history of helping. Strong-Thorne and Fitzgerald and Son look forward and will continue to serve families into the new millennium.

1100 Coal Avenue SE, Albuquerque, NM 87106, 842-8800

The Strong brothers didn't know they would become founders of a five-generation tradition.

the Spirit of
BANK OF AMERICA est. 1924

Consider the comfort of dealing with a local bank, where the staff members (who live and work in Albuquerque) provide exceptional service, and where products and prices are convenient and competitively priced. A bank whose people enthusiastically support the whole life of the Albuquerque community: local schools, youth soccer, the arts, health and human services, and the under-served. A neighborhood institution with integrity and character and a long history of serving its friends and neighbors.

Now, consider the even greater satisfaction that comes from knowing your bank also provides you with the choice, convenience and coast-to-coast access of nationwide banking.

As a businessperson, consider the benefits of working with a financial services organization that can meet all of your financial needs. One that offers tremendous resources to small and mid-sized businesses, corporations and government agencies. An organi-zation that delivers capacity and product breadth, global reach and superior execution through teams of talented banking professionals.

As an individual customer, a bank that offers products and services for every financial need no matter how you choose to manage your money. A bank that lets you bank how, when and where you want – in person, or from any telephone or computer terminal in the state or in the world.

Finally, consider that all these accomplishments are just the beginning. This company – Bank of America – is determined to be much more. Bank of America is building a company that makes banking work for customers in ways it never has before. A bank reshaped around those things that matter most to our individual and business customers: convenience, simplic-ity, flexibility and depend-ability. A bank that continues to be a strong partner and able leader in the Albuquerque community.

Bank of America is building America's bank of the future.

303 Roma Avenue NW, Albuquerque, NM 87102, 282-2106, www.bankofamerica.com

the Spirit of
BFGOODRICH AEROSPACE est. 1954

Engineering high-technology applications for outer space is the business of BFGoodrich Aerospace in Albuquerque. The company develops and manufactures custom devices for use in a most challenging environment: their products have applications for clients like NASA, the military and telecommunications. After nearly 50 years of launching failure-free electronic subsystems into space, BFGoodrich Aerospace believes high reliability is a huge factor in their success.

BFGoodrich's engineering and development capabilities have created an amazing array of electronic subsystems with highly techni-cal applications. The Total Ozone Mapping Spectrometer (TOMS-EP), launched in July 1996 aboard a TRW Earth Probe Satellite, has mapped in detail the global ozone distribution and the Antarctic "ozone hole" that forms every September. The TOMS-EP also meas-ures the sulfur dioxide released in volcanic eruptions. It is part of NASA's Mission to Planet Earth, a long-term, coordinated research effort to study the global environment.

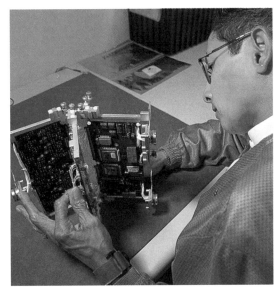

BFGoodrich Aerospace's Data Systems Division has devised electronic systems for the Chandra Experiment (a mission to explore the origin of our universe), the National Missile Defense Program and an upgrade of the Global Positioning System (GPS), to name a few. This division also developed the Telemetry Encoder Unit for the Transfer Orbit Stage of the Mars Observer spacecraft, a mapping satellite that conducts topography, mineralogy and climatology studies of Mars. Data Systems Division also provides electronic subsystems for some of the world's pre-mier launch vehicles including Delta, Atlas and Sea Launch.

With sales approaching $4 billion, BFGoodrich Aerospace is one of the world's leading suppliers of aerospace components and systems. Its manufacturing operation capabilities are quantitative and comprehensive. The Data Systems Division employs more than 450 people in Albuquerque. From the first pressure suit that enabled pilots to fly at 30,000 feet to NASA's Space Shuttle, and beyond, BFGoodrich Aerospace is proud of its rich heritage and its bright future of leading the space industry into the next millennium.

6600 Gulton Court NE, Albuquerque, NM 87109, 345-9031, www.bfg-aerospace.com

▶ Satellite Assembly II— Printed Card Assembly (PCA) manufacturing is an integral part of product success. Soldering for space applications is highly critical to performance.

Satellite Assembly I— Final unit inter-wiring is critical for each PCA to electronically talk to each other for product system success. Units can have up to 25 interwired PCAs and up to 4,000 individual wires.

the Spirit of
KPMG LLP est. 1956

KPMG reaffirms its far-reaching commitments every day. To education, by co-sponsoring Computers for Kids, becoming a Join-A-School Partner and volunteering for Junior Achievement. To the arts, by sponsoring Salsa Under the Stars and concerts by the New Mexico Symphony Orchestra. To health, by participating in events for the American Cancer Society and the March of Dimes. To local agencies, like the Albuquerque Department of Senior Affairs. To economic evolution, by bringing companies through start-up to development to growth. And to work-force development, by hiring graduates of UNM and NMSU.

▶ KPMG LLP's management group — partners and managers from Albuquerque — are a small but vital part of the whole. There are over 75 KPMG people in Albuquerque alone.

Located in Albuquerque since 1956, KPMG brings international resources in accounting, tax and business consulting to New Mexico. As a member of one of the world's leading professional services firms, KPMG brings the depth and breadth of those services to local businesses, universities, Native Americans, financial institutions, publicly-held companies, the health-care industry, and city, state and federal agencies. From multi-state to multi-national accounting advice, tax services and strategies, to Internet-based services, technology applications transfer and global e-commerce, KPMG brings its expertise to New Mexico's fingertips.

KPMG touches the people here, too. Every member of the management group serves on the boards of various organizations including the Chamber of Commerce, Habitat for Humanity, United Way, All Faiths Receiving Home, Albuquerque Boys and Girls Club, Anderson Schools, Better Business Bureau, Economic Forum and Albuquerque Economic Development. KPMG's alumni include business owners, CEOs, CFOs, COOs, citizens of consequence and respected competitors. "Working at KPMG prepares people to be leaders in business and the community," says Gary Dushane, managing partner. "It's one more way we contribute to Albuquerque's growth and prosperity." Albuquerque agrees.

"Working at KPMG prepares people to be leaders in business and the community."

6565 Americas Parkway NE, Suite 700, Albuquerque, NM 87190, 884-3939, www.us.kpmg.com

2
6
4

the spirit of
TALBOT AGENCY, INC. est. 1957

Insurance is a critical element in any city's business infrastructure and Albuquerque is fortunate to be the hometown of an outstanding insurance agency. Talbot Agency, Inc., employs over 700 people and is the second-largest broker headquartered in the western United States. In addition to being a resource to the city's businesses and families, Talbot is itself a true Albuquerque success story.

Founded in 1957 as a one-man agency by Lyle Talbot, the operation grew along with the city. Specialty services were added to the core insurance operations. Talbot Financial Services is now one of the nation's leading distributors of annuities and mutual funds, with annual sales in excess of $1 billion. Under CEO David Weymouth, Talbot recently opened its 58th office in its 19th state.

For businesses in Albuquerque, Talbot offers unmatched resources, expertise and industry influence. As an independent agency, Talbot represents over 100 highly-rated insurance carriers. In addition to property, liability and workers' compensation coverages, the agency provides specialized business insurance coverages and surety and bonding services. Plans and programs that are uniquely New Mexican are delivered by its employee benefits department. Homeowners, auto and umbrella coverages are available from the personal insurance department, which also insures vacation homes and custom-designs plans to manage estate-level risks.

Talbot's commitment to Albuquerque is deep and enduring. Employees lend their individual time and expertise to scores of worthy causes, and year after year the company increases its collective efforts to help the United Way and other community agencies. Talbot is a founding member of the United Way's Corporate Cornerstone Program.

By being consummate professionals, and helping to ensure the financial well-being of Albuquerque's businesses and families, Talbot helps make the city an even more attractive place to live and work.

▶ Pictured, from left: Stu Kuyper, Executive Vice President (Southwest Region); David E. Weymouth, President & CEO; Robin Schritter, Vice President (Personal Insurance); Dan Scott, Senior Vice President (Employee Benefits).

2
6
5

Founded in 1957 as a one-man agency, Talbot now employs over 700 people.

7770 Jefferson Boulevard NE, Albuquerque, NM 87109, 828-4000 or 800-800-5661, www.talbotcorp.com

Within the foundations of every city, beneath the feet of its citizens and the walls of its buildings, lies a solid base of concrete. Made in part of aggregate and water, concrete cannot become solid without its bonding agent, cement. For concrete, cement is the adhesive that holds it all together. The resulting substance is the premier ingredient in bridges and buildings, sidewalks and highways.

Within a corporation, its leader becomes the catalyst for change and growth, the one who provides the solid foundations of a thriving enterprise. For Rio Grande Portland Cement Corporation, that leader is Oscar Del Valle, President and Chief Executive Officer. He is the leader of an organization that has become the cornerstone for the construction industry in Albuquerque and the only cement manufacturing plant in New Mexico. The company supplies cement to redi-mix producers and concrete block manufacturers statewide, delivering superlative service and a quality product. Under Mr. Del Valle's guidance, Rio Grande Portland Cement has become an important part of the economic infrastructure of the City of Albuquerque.

Rio Grande Portland Cement employs 70 people at its Tijeras plant, most of whom live in Albuquerque. Using gypsum and iron ore mined near Capitan, coal ash from Prewitt and sand from other parts of the state, the corporation buys resources contained within New Mexico borders. An enormous energy capacity is needed to run a cement plant 24 hours a day, 365 days a year, which makes Rio Grande Portland Cement one of the largest customers of Public Service Company of New Mexico. Rio Grande Portland has completed installation of computerized power usage controls that regulate energy consumed for peak operating efficiency and keep the air surrounding the facility clean and dust-free.

Rio Grande Portland Cement Corporation has become a leading part of the economic life of Albuquerque; their strategic plans for growth will

Rio Grande Portland Cement is an important part of Albuquerque's economic infrastructure.

serve the city, the great state of New Mexico and Rio Grande Portland Cement Corp. well into the next century.

4253 Montgomery Boulevard NE, Albuquerque, NM 87109, 881-5304, www.gcc.com

Tijeras plant, Tijeras, New Mexico.

Oscar Del Valle, President & CEO.

266

Higher education – or hire education. Whichever way you look at it, Albuquerque Technical Vocational Institute (TVI) has for nearly 35 years helped to build Albuquerque's work force. Today, TVI boasts a 96 percent job placement rate for its graduates, who are now employed at large and small businesses throughout the region.

"Job training is at the heart of our mission," says TVI President Michael J. Glennon. "Helping local residents gain the skills needed to succeed in today's fast-paced, high-tech world is what we do best. This applies to all of our students, whether they're here to earn an occupational certificate or degree, take classes to upgrade their skills or transfer to a university."

▶ Albuquerque TVI's main campus occupies 60 acres near downtown.

TVI's focus on work-force training has sharpened with its new Workforce Training Center. Catering to business and industry, the center offers job training for area employers; assessment services to help companies identify their training needs; and a Small Business Development Center to help grow new and existing small companies. The center is in the heart of Albuquerque's growing I-25 industrial corridor.

Founded in 1965, TVI is a comprehensive community college offering occupational, college transfer and adult/developmental education

Welding is just one of TVI's many hands-on job-training programs

programs. Programs include: certificates in 45 business, health, technologies and trades occupations; associate degrees in 35 occupational fields and liberal arts; college transfer courses in pre-management, pre-engineering and other occupational subjects, along with 23 liberal arts disciplines; and adult/developmental education classes, including basic skills, ESL and GED exam preparation.

With an enrollment of 23,000, TVI is the second-largest post-secondary institution in the state. To serve the greater Albuquerque area, the Institute has four campuses: the Main Campus near downtown, the Joseph M. Montoya Campus in the Northeast Heights, and two smaller campuses in Rio Rancho and the South Valley. TVI is accredited by the Commission on Institutions of Higher Education of the North Central Association of Colleges and Schools.

"Helping residents gain the skills to succeed in today's high-tech world is what we do best."

525 Buena Vista Drive SE, Albuquerque, NM 87106, 224-3000, www.tvi.cc.nm.us

▶

Albuquerque International Sunport.

BPLW Architects & Engineers, Inc., provides architectural, civil, structural, mechanical and electrical engineering and has helped form New Mexico's built landscape for more than 30 years. With more than 115 employees and four offices throughout the Southwest, including headquarters' office in Albuquerque, BPLW offers multi-discipline professional services for clients in government, the military, education and high technology.

BPLW's high-profile projects include the new $40 million Consolidated Rental Car Facility near the Albuquerque International Sunport that will house nine agencies on 76 acres. A new project for AT&T features project management for the location, site adaptation and construction of area telephone structures within New Mexico, Nevada, Arizona and Texas. Recently, BPLW completed a $12 million design/build project on a Flight Simulator for Kirtland Air Force Base.

Complex design/build projects require teams of architects and engineers to see them through, on time and on budget. At BPLW, those teams are in-house, serving the customer with one-stop project management. BPLW's range of design/build expertise also supports designer-led projects, a unique capability that defines their flexibility and the extent of their services.

**The Board of Directors.
Seated:
Ronald L. Peters,
Bill J. Waters,
William L. Burns.
Standing:
Maureen M. Walter,
W. Paul Waters,
Eugene A. Valentine,
Charlie M. Otero,
John C. Crafton,
Bruce A. Schneider.
Not pictured:
Guy C. Jackson and
David A. Penasa.**

Other architectural, engineering and design/build highlights include projects for the University of New Mexico and New Mexico State University, and New Mexico Tech; and 10 new post offices for the United States Postal Service.

BPLW continues to receive numerous awards and accolades for their designs. They have been repeatedly recognized in the Top 500 Professional Design Firms in the U.S. by *Engineering News Record Magazine*. *Building Design and Construction Magazine* has included BPLW among their top 50 architectural and engineering firms since 1991.

BPLW also supports designer-led projects, a unique capability that defines their flexibility.

6200 Uptown Boulevard, Suite 400, Albuquerque, NM 87110, 881-2759, www.bplw.com

the Spirit of
LOCKHEED MARTIN CORPORATION est. 1969

For decades, Lockheed Martin and New Mexico have been working in partnership to build a stronger business base. Lockheed Martin's commitment to New Mexico extends directly into the heart of the community through education and cultural programs, economic development initiatives and social services.

Sandia Corporation, a Lockheed Martin company, manages Sandia National Laboratories for the Department of Energy. For 50 years, Sandia has provided scientific and engineering solutions to meet the nation's defense, energy and environmental needs. Technology Ventures Corporation (TVC) is a non-profit corporation founded by Lockheed Martin to facilitate the commercialization of laboratory technologies, creating private-sector jobs.

Lockheed Martin takes its commitment seriously. It is New Mexico's largest employer, with over 9,400 employees statewide. Each year, their payroll pumps more than $640 million directly into the economy; they purchase more than $260 million in goods and services; and they pay the state more than $50 million in gross receipts taxes.

TVC has facilitated the creation of 36 new technology businesses, generating over 1,900 New Mexico jobs, and bringing in over $140 million in investment capital to our state.

The employees of Sandia and TVC have contributed more than $15 million to the United Way of Central New Mexico over the last decade. Those employees have volunteered over 300,000 hours of community service in support of many worthy organizations.

Lockheed Martin has donated nearly $3.5 million to educational initiatives including New Mexico's Math and Science Academy, the New Mexico Museum of Natural History, the Rocket Reader program and the National Atomic Museum Capital Campaign.

Lockheed Martin has donated an additional $1.5 million to organizations including the Greater Albuquerque Chamber of Commerce, the Hispano Cultural Center, Make a Wish Foundation, the Albuquerque Public Schools Foundation, Habitat for Humanity and the Albuquerque Public Aquarium.

One Technology Center, 1155 University Boulevard SE, Albuquerque, NM 87106, 246-2882

Children exploring the Lockheed Martin Corporation shark tank at the Albuquerque Aquarium.

Members of the Anthony Rael family enter their new home, built by the Lockheed Martin Corporation and Habitat for Humanity.

Lockheed Martin's commitment to New Mexico extends into the heart of the community.

269

the Spirit of
ATKINSON & CO., LTD. est. 1970

270

Throughout the life of a thriving business, you'll always find a guiding hand at the helm. Every business needs a trusted advisor, that elder statesman who becomes the informal chairman of the board, an expert mentor upon whose advice they rely. When that advisor can navigate the tricky course of a firm's financial evolution, the value of their counsel increases.

Atkinson & Co., Ltd., certified public accountants and consultants, takes a client by the hand and leads the way through growth and succession, mergers and acquisitions, all the phases of a company's life. Step by step, they maintain a close and steady relationship to see your company through the rough and the smooth. Atkinson & Co. has steered its loyal clients through every type of transition, from stasis to growth, from start-up to investment capital, from generation to generation. It's no surprise that they have kept many of the same clients for more than 30 years.

Atkinson & Co. cultivates other relationships, too, to team with bankers and lawyers, business and community leaders, to give your business the full-service support it needs to flourish. One important relationship is the affiliation of Atkinson & Co. with Moore Stephens. Moore Stephens Atkinson LLC is the national and international arm of the company, extending its worldwide consulting and accounting services to clients with a need for global guidance. A small accounting and consulting firm can give your company care and attention. A large firm can offer services that small CPAs can't provide. At Atkinson & Co., you get the benefit of both: meticulous, individualized attention coupled with the professional services of an international consortium.

There's something different here. That's the company catchphrase that inspires the 65 employees at Atkinson & Co. to give big company service and small company care to loyal clients who recognize that Atkinson & Co. is a leader within the business community of Albuquerque.

Atkinson & Co. leads the way through all the phases of a company's life.

707 Broadway Boulevard NE, Suite 400, Albuquerque, NM 87102, 843-6492

the spirit of
BUSINESS ENVIRONMENTS est. 1973

Business Environments (BE) is New Mexico's largest office furnishings and commercial floor-coverings firm. Founded in 1973, the Albuquerque-based company is currently managed by brothers Bruce and Scott Hoover. During the past 26 years, this local, family-owned business has grown from three to over 70 full-time employees. The company's success is attributed to its long-standing philosophy of employing the best people and providing solutions to their clients' needs with the ultimate objective being total customer satisfaction.

▶ Business Environments Executive Committee (from left): I.B. Hoover, Bruce Hoover, Joe Chandler, Rick Ailts, Scott Hoover.

BE has built their reputation by providing high quality products and services that have an everlasting value to their clients. Their expertise is in providing interior solutions that enhance workplace performance and conserve office space.

BE's clients range from two- to three-person offices to major corporate clients. Their diversified client list results from their desire and ability to provide professional office furnishings, floor coverings and services to any entity that is seeking to improve its office environment. Companies representing banking and finance, high-tech manufacturing, the legal profession, health care and telecommunications, to name just a few, provide an impressive mix of clientele who have found solutions to their needs by working with BE.

Steelcase is the world's largest manufacturer of quality office furnishing. For the past 26 years, BE has represented Steelcase throughout the state of New Mexico. In addition, for many years the company has represented Milliken and Shaw, two of the most respected and reputable manufacturers of floor coverings. During 1998 the company added a medium-priced furniture division, Office Furniture USA, to accommodate the growing office furniture requirements for medium, small and start-up businesses.

You are invited to contact BE to discuss any needs that involve your office. Consultation with BE can provide workable, affordable solutions that will enhance personnel productivity, improve morale and have a positive impact on the bottom line of your company.

> BE has built their reputation by providing products and services with an everlasting value.

4121 Prospect Avenue NE, Albuquerque, NM 87110, 888-4400, www.businessenvironments.com

the spirit of
ALBUQUERQUE TITLE COMPANY, INC. est. 1976

Growing as New Mexico grows, Albuquerque Title Company began here nearly 25 years ago as a small local firm that now employs 80 people and is one of the largest title companies in the state. Now operating as a direct subsidiary of LandAmerica Financial Group, a nationwide family of companies whose mission supports commercial real estate investment and home ownership. Albuquerque Title Company and its employees are dedicated to the efficient transfer of real estate and the protection of those interests.

▶ Albuquerque Title employees are proud supporters of Habitat for Humanity.

Beyond those business goals, Albuquerque Title Company puts their time, efforts and money on the line to support local charitable organizations and non-profits. Their employees are encouraged to participate in events and community groups that benefit children and their families such as Joy Junction, Peanut Butter & Jelly Preschool and Habitat for Humanity. Recently, employees teamed up for a canned food drive competition to benefit Joy Junction. Every year they participate in various activities for Habit for Humanity and collect toys for the Peanut Butter & Jelly Preschool at Christmas. Such dedication to community and team spirit must agree with them, for over half of the employees have been with the company in excess of 15 years.

President Carolyn Monroe and other senior management devote much of their own time and energy to volunteer work for related industry associations. Ms. Monroe has served on the Board of Directors for Albuquerque Economic Development, the National Association of Industrial and Office Properties, Economic Forum, the New Mexico Land Title Association and the Albuquerque Chamber of Commerce. A company with national power behind it, Albuquerque Title Company backs up its local presence with community and professional involvement that embraces Albuquerque's most cherished and vital institutions.

Albuquerque Title Company backs up its local presence with community involvement.

2400 Louisiana Boulevard NE, Building 5, Albuquerque, NM 87110, 883-9595

272

the spirit of COTTONWOOD PRINTING est. 1978

273

In printing, excellence is now a given. If it isn't right, it isn't right, and "good enough" is no longer acceptable! Every aspect of the printed product, from initial customer contact to final delivery, must exceed the customer's expectation. When a printing company turns out a perfect job, well, that's simply what the customer expects.

Cottonwood Printing goes beyond perfect jobs — they continue to improve the process to exceed customer expectations, because that is what the customer doesn't expect. Cottonwood boasts one of the finest electronic pre-press departments in the state. Their skilled personnel is always pre-pared to facilitate the client's needs. Cottonwood Printing's multi-shift structure ensures your proofs and projects are available to you on time. Cottonwood is the only printing company to have won the Piñon Award presented by Quality New Mexico.

▶ Team involvement is encouraged and practiced at Cottonwood Printing. Team members meet regularly to plan, review and critique the company's process.

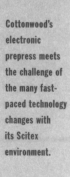

Along with customer satisfaction, the employees of Cottonwood realize their responsibility to the environment and the community they live in. Cottonwood Printing Company is committed to minimizing the impact of its production process on the environ-ment. Aggressive waste reduction, material recycling and using chemicals with the least environmental impact are just some of the actions taken by Cottonwood Printing. Cottonwood was very pleased to have received one of the first Green Zia Achievement Awards presented by the State of New Mexico Environment Department for its efforts to be "green" and "clean."

Cottonwood's electronic prepress meets the challenge of the many fast-paced technology changes with its Scitex environment.

Cottonwood Printing is proudest of their employees' enthusiasm and commit-ment to the company's vision. There is a mock-up of a rocket ship in the employee's break room depicting the department's action plans to achieve the company's goals, and it is headed for the moon. It is a fitting symbol of Cottonwood's focus and outlook, of a company that always takes that surprising next step to zoom above and beyond customer expectations.

Cottonwood Printing continues to improve their process to exceed customer expectations.

2117 Osuna Road NE, Albuquerque, NM 87113, 345-5341, www.cottonwoodprint.com

Intel is a kingpin among computer chip and component manufacturers, but it also prides itself on being a good corporate neighbor and community partner. Through its dedication to education, volunteerism and community service, the company has made New Mexico a better place to live – and work.

From a staff of 25 employees in 1980, Intel has grown to more than 5,000, making it one of the largest private employers in the state. And the company makes a strong effort to hire from within the community – about 66 percent of its new hires come from inside the state.

▶ **About 70 percent of Intel New Mexico employees are manufacturing technicians who work in "clean-rooms," which are thousands of times cleaner than a hospital operating room.**

With a goal of providing jobs for New Mexicans, the company has invested a great deal in education, improving schools and providing incentives to increase the skills and knowledge of the New Mexican work force. Among other contributions, Intel has donated $30 million for the construction of Rio Rancho High School, contributed $1 million to TVI for the creation of a cleanroom training lab and donated $1.7 million in equipment to the UNM College of Engineering. The company has also invested more than $7 million to develop two-year degree programs at New Mexico community colleges.

In 1999, more than 1,400 Intel employees donated more than 27,000 hours of volunteer time to community service projects.

"We're strongly involved in education, particularly in science and math curricula," says Bill Garcia, the public affairs manager for Intel in New Mexico. "Our desire is to improve our community while also meeting an Intel need for promoting those skills in a potential work force." The company also promotes volunteerism among its employees, who have dedicated their time and energy to scores of non-profit organizations. In 1999, Intel and its employees donated more than $720,000 to the United Way, leading the way in a citywide campaign. "Our company and its employees actively donate their time, resources and commitment to local organizations, supporting a wide range of activities," Garcia says. "We're very proud of that. I think that speaks well of Intel as a corporate citizen."

> "Our employees actively donate their time and resources to local organizations."

4100 Sara Road, Rio Rancho, NM 87124, 893-7000, www.intel.com

274

the spirit of
RAINBOW RYDERS, INC. est. 1982

Beautiful hot-air balloons dotting the sky have become as intricately connected to New Mexico's image and culture as green chile and enchantment, and Rainbow Ryders, Inc., wants everyone – from locals to visitors – to be able to experience that magic. Since 1982 Rainbow Ryders' founder, Scott Appelman, and his wife, Liz Appelman, have been using their vast experience and knowledge to help people enjoy year-round rides in the elegant and graceful airships.

▶ Part of Rainbow Ryder's colorful fleet.

Rainbow Ryders has been involved in many aspects of ballooning across the state and the country. Scott Appelman holds the world altitude record for ballooning, at 24,680 feet, and co-founded the Special Shape Rodeo® and the Balloon Glow® at the Kodak™ Albuquerque International Balloon Fiesta, where the company is the official ride concessionaire. In addition, the Appelmans and other company staff have flown custom balloons for several corporations – including Ocean Spray Cranberry Juice,

General Mills, Gateway Computers and KOB-TV – in events across the country.

The company also won the Tourism Company of the Year award from the Albuquerque Convention and Visitors Bureau, but "the biggest award we get is getting to do the balloon fiesta each year and to show people how special balloon rides really are," Scott Appelman says.

Scott and Liz Appelman aboard one of their hot-air ballon gondolas.

By allowing its customers to participate in as much or as little of the ballooning process as they'd like – from inflating the balloon to flying – Rainbow Ryders gives a hands-on, in-depth ballooning experience. And when it's all over, customers enjoy a champagne toast and receive a balloon flight certificate and pin.

"We try to make our balloon rides special to people," Scott Appelman says. "We personalize the service, realizing that 99 percent of our customers will only go for one balloon ride in their life – and we want to make that something really fantastic."

"The biggest award we get is getting to show people how special balloon rides really are."

11520 San Bernadino Drive NE, Albuquerque, NM 87122, 823-1111, www.rainbowryders.com

the Spirit of
PHILIPS SEMICONDUCTORS est. 1983

One of the world's largest manufacturers of semiconductors, Philips has a chip-making facility the size of 10 football fields on 62 acres in the I-25 corridor. The plant was opened in 1982 and employs approximately 1,000 people in the areas of design, testing, manufacturing, support and administration. It is one of the largest manufacturing plants of any type in New Mexico, and one of the largest employers in the state. Philips Semiconductors in Albuquerque manufactures integrated circuits used in products around the world. These tiny but powerful electronic devices are manufactured here for use in computers and peripherals, cars, TVs, VCRs and cellular phones. Philips Semiconductors entire division worldwide operates 15 manufacturing and assembly sites in 10 countries and employs more than 27,000 people.

Philips Semiconductors is considerate to its neighbors and to the environment. They planned and participate in the I-25 Industrial Water Recycling Project in partnership with the City of Albuquerque and their corporate neighbors. This system recycles wastewater from the manufacturing of silicon chips for irrigation and industrial use in the Alameda/North I-25 area. Philips Semiconductors originally came up with the idea of the recycling project, earning it the name "the Philips Plan."

In 1999 the Albuquerque plant received a Green Zia Environmental Excellence Award from the State of New Mexico's Department of the Environment. In 1998 Philips won the World Environment Center's Gold Medal Award for International Corporate Environmental Achievement. The Albuquerque plant has received the U.S. Environmental Protection Agency's Environmental Excellence Award four times and the EPA's Compliance Plus Award twice, the only manufacturing plant in the country to be so honored. A world leader in the development and use of digital technologies for sophis-

ticated consumer products, Philips Semiconductors brings up-to-the-minute, ecologically-sound technologies to Albuquerque.

Philips manufactures integrated circuits used in products around the world.

9201 Pan American Freeway NE, Albuquerque, NM 87113, 822-7000, www.abq.sc.philips.com

the Spirit of
MEYNERS + COMPANY, LLC est. 1983

Many companies rely on accountants who take a traditional approach to planning for the future. They tend to assist you by looking in the rearview mirror while your organization is lurching forward.

Today's business environment requires business consultants and accounting firms that are visionaries, innovators and futurists. They look beyond the horizon and help you assess the risks of getting you where you want to go.

This new breed of business advisor is blazing trails right here in Albuquerque. Meyners + Company, LLC, is a nationally-recognized accounting and consulting firm that has built its reputation on creating and implementing innovative strategies for forward-thinking organizations. As a member of the BDO Seidman Alliance, Meyners + Company combines the personal interaction of a local firm with the resources of one of the world's largest accounting and consulting organizations. "We look beyond standard accounting approaches to uncover new ideas for improving business operations and increasing profitability," says Bruce Malott, Managing Principal. "We can cut through complex matters, like business valuation and profit enhancement, with up-to-the-minute expertise that helps you visualize your business' growth, then achieve it."

Meyners + Company's six principals have over 115 years of combined experience. From left to right: Tom Burrage, Jeff Burns, Bruce Malott (Managing Principal), Reta Jones, Kirk Flanagan, Brandon Hill Haines.

Providing exceptional client service is Meyners + Company's top priority. The firm has received numerous national awards for excellence in client service and practice management.

Meyners + Company's full range of business and strategic financial services leverages its business know-how and a wide array of resources. Its more than 60 professionals can provide expertise in specialized areas such as Litigation Support and Business Valuation; Audit; Technology Applications; Business Services; Employee Benefits Services; Financial and Estate Planning; and Tax Planning and Compliance. They can also augment the efforts of your in-house professionals to provide solid expertise in areas ranging from practice management to expert witness testimony to managing massive amounts of data. From providing seamless software and hardware solutions to proactive consulting and problem solving, they'll show you how to steer your business toward its own profitable future.

You've always had a vision for your company. Meyners + Company can help you get there.

"We look past standard accounting approaches to uncover new ideas for improving operations."

500 Marquette Avenue NW, Suite 400, Albuquerque, NM 87102, 842-8290, www.meyners.com

the spirit of
DESIGN COLLABORATIVE SOUTHWEST ARCHITECTS, INC. est. 1984

"Form and function should be one, joined in a spiritual union." Frank Lloyd Wright said it, and he might have been speaking of the creative projects of Design Collaborative Southwest. For if a building can be said to have a soul, DCSW has the skill and style to seamlessly blend design and function for their clients in any setting.

Design Collaborative Southwest, Inc., was founded in 1984, its mission to create architecture that embodies

▶ The 70,000-square-foot N.M. Farm and Ranch Heritage Museum in Las Cruces, NM, exemplifies DCSW's emphasis on design for local context and culture.

excellence and innovation in design, energy efficiency, and economic value. DCSW has had the opportunity to work with clients as diverse as the United

States Air Force, Lockheed Martin and MCI. Their work for the Navajo Nation includes the Diné Museum and Seba Dalkai Boarding School, a complex that echoes the children's cultural heritage in its site plan, buildings and interior motifs. The DCSW-designed Metropolitan Court building in Albuquerque incorporates high-tech functions like video visitation in an atmosphere of dignity and customer service. Public-use buildings like the South Broadway Library and

DCSW staff stands in front of the flagship of Lockheed Martin in Albuquerque, the TVC Center. This 65,000-square-foot corporate office, designed by DCSW, was awarded 1995 Building of the Year by NAIOP.

the new Lodestar/I-Werks Theatre at the Museum of Natural History and Science combine ideal beauty with state-of-the-art technology, so well do DCSW's architects understand how the uses of those buildings fit the needs of their community.

DCSW's team approach affords their clients access to the creative efforts of all members of the firm, and characterizes DCSW's full investment in client objectives. The 35-person staff is committed to innova-

tive design vision, cost-effectiveness and exemplary service. The firm provides architecture, planning, interior design, historic preservation and passive solar design throughout New Mexico and the western states. DCSW has received 47

significant design awards in 15 years, a testament to their passion, mastery and vision of the practice of architecture and how it touches lives and souls.

DCSW has the technical skill to blend design and function for their clients in any setting.

320 Central Avenue SW, Albuquerque, NM 87102, 843-9639, www.dcswarchitects.com

the Spirit of
SBS TECHNOLOGIES est. 1986

For some companies, learning to shift gears in the ever-changing high-tech computer market is a difficult task, but SBS Technologies thrives on it. Founded in Albuquerque in late 1986, SBS has transformed itself from a small flight simulator manufacturer for the defense industry to one of the five largest computer board and system manufacturers in the world in only a few short years.

"Refocus-reward" is one of the mantras of Christopher Amenson, Chairman of the Board and CEO of SBS. And since Amenson came to the company in 1992, that's just what he's been doing, refocusing the company's energy into emerging high-tech markets and expanding SBS' range of products through acquisition and development.

Over the years, the company has shifted and broadened its focus from military flight applications to the $7 billion computer board industry. Since going public in 1992, SBS has acquired seven companies that have helped expand its product line and its ability to function in a multitude of computer environments. Currently, SBS provides over 400 products, including customized computer boards, I/O boards, whole computer systems and software for such impressive customers as General Electric, Eastman Kodak, Boeing, TRW, Raytheon, Lucent and Disney Imagineering. They even have manufactured boards to function in the harsh environment of space.

The company also has expanded its marketplace, with offices in California, Minnesota, North Carolina and Germany. But it also hasn't forgotten its roots – SBS still has its corporate headquarters and Aerospace Group located here in Albuquerque. The city's proximity to the labs, the ability for a company to work in the state's geopolitical environment and, most of all, the beautiful weather and scenery make Albuquerque a fine home for his company, Amenson says.

"I think we've created something special with this company, and I'm glad we're right here in New Mexico," he says.

AFC-5, 2400 Louisiana Boulevard NE, Suite 600, Albuquerque, NM, 87110, 875-0600, www.sbs.com

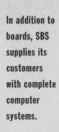

SBS supports its complete line of embedded computer boards with extensive software.

In addition to boards, SBS supplies its customers with complete computer systems.

the Spirit of
ALBUQUERQUE TORTILLA COMPANY est. 1987

2 8 0

As a small-time chile salesman, Luther Martinez often left his customers with the same complaint ringing in his ears. A homestyle tortilla could not be found.

Settling down with a used tortilla machine, a secret recipe and a dream, Luther Martinez began to fulfill his customers' requests. The eight employees in the tiny building on Fourth Street, along with Luther and his wife, Rose, did not even begin to fathom the stir they would soon be causing in the New Mexican food industry.

Since 1987 Albuquerque Tortilla Company has outgrown many locations and will soon house the company in 105,000 square feet of space. Together, with the help of state-of-the-art tortilla making machinery, Albuquerque Tortilla Company's 170 employees are turning out 300,000 dozen tortillas weekly. Many of those tortillas are then distributed by the company's six semi trailers throughout the Southwest and the West Coast. Two wholesale outlets serve local caterers and restaurants who prefer to pick up their own tortillas at a wholesale discount.

Nobody can compare with Albuquerque Tortilla Company's "Homestyle" brand of tortillas. The company, adamant in giving the customer what they want, also manufactures corn tortillas. Vegetable Products, Inc., of Salem, New Mexico, supplies the company with frozen Hatch green chile and freshly ground spices used in the company's chile rellenos and tamales.

Luther and Rose Martinez, native New Mexicans, feel the support they have received from the city and its citizens have been an important part in making their company an Albuquerque success story. Their two children, Chris and Tammy, work in the business as well, a promise that Albuquerque Tortilla Company's customers will continue to enjoy the secret-recipe tortillas for generations to come.

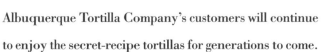

Support from the city and its citizens has made Albuquerque Tortilla Company a success story.

4300 Alexander Boulevard NE, Albuquerque, NM 87107, 344-4011, www.albuquerquetortilla.com

the spirit of
ALLEGIANCE HEALTHCARE est. 1988

When Allegiance Healthcare started looking for a location to expand its successful medical products business, it fell in love with Albuquerque – the city, its people and its business-friendly environment. The company has been here, partnered with the community, since 1988, and it sees a bright future for both itself and for New Mexico. "I love the creativity of the people here," says Kevin Smith, Vice President and General Manager of Allegiance. "The culture of diversity is wonderful. It just makes for a great work environment. The spirit of the people here is really something unique."

▶ The Allegiance Shared Services Employee team.

Allegiance is the leader in distributing medical, surgical and laboratory products to hospitals and other health-care providers. In addition, it is a company full of opportunity, often promoting employees who started at entry-level positions onto its managerial staff. Allegiance, which was once part of Baxter International, Inc., recently merged with Cardinal Healthcare, making it one of the largest medical supplies companies in the world. Before the merger Allegiance had 19,800 employees worldwide and 450 employees in its

By integrating skill in distribution and manufacturing with a range of cost-management services, Allegiance is differentiating itself as the company best able to help hospitals. and others in health care save money and focus on patient care rather than supplies and logistics.

Albuquerque Allegiance financial center, which handles credit collections, accounts payable and contract administration. By partnering with Cardinal, the company hopes to create even more new jobs for the Albuquerque community.

"We believe there's going to be greater opportunity, because merging with a company that has $21 billion in sales is going to create more jobs," Smith says. "And we have the facilities set up here in Albuquerque to be able to provide support for those sales."

The company also believes in a strong commitment to local charities, and has made contributions to a number of associations, including the March of Dimes, the United Way, AIDS Walk and Junior Achievement. In addition, Allegiance provides educational support to the community through participation with Albuquerque TVI's Workforce Training Center.

"The culture of diversity is wonderful. The spirit of the people here is something unique."

4200 Osuna Road NE, Albuquerque, NM 87109, 761-1000, www.allegiance.net

the Spirit of
HIGH DESERT est. 1991

High Desert is a community like no other in the greater Albuquerque area. Just a short drive from downtown, High Desert is a world away, demonstrating that a beautiful development can responsibly coexist with nature.

Located in the foothills of the Sandia Mountains, High Desert is designed to function in harmony with its natural surroundings. By using innovative development techniques outlined in its Guidelines for Sustainability, High Desert has created a special place for the people of Albuquerque to live.

"Through much of the community we have preserved the natural landforms," says Douglas Collister, president of High Desert. "We've also kept a third of the land area as open space of one kind or another. There are hiking trails, biking trails and walking trails throughout." In addition, High Desert has enhanced the vegetation and increased the wildlife habitat in many of the remnant arroyos so they will function as buffers,

protecting the natural surroundings. High Desert also uses water-harvesting techniques, allows a limited number of wood-burning fireplaces and has light pollution standards to help protect the fragile environment.

High Desert offers a wide variety of custom home sites ranging in size from 1/3 acre to 2 acres, each of which offers stunning views of the city and the mountains. The community also features 12 different neighborhood villages, with homes ranging from 1,100 square feet to over 5,000 square feet. These and many other community amenities can be previewed on its website at www.high-desert.com.

"Each of the villages has a distinct kind of personality to it and character with certain sizes, prices and styles," Collister says. "We're trying to create a special place here that we can look back on and take pride in as members of the larger Albuquerque community."

"We're creating a place that we can take pride in as members of the larger community."

13000 Academy Road NE, Albuquerque, NM 87111, 823-9360, www. high-desert.com

Employees of Rio Grande Medical Technologies would have a lot to write home about if they weren't already home. But Albuquerque is home to the 70 men and women of a company that is leading the way in research and quality of life both on and off the job. RGMT was founded in Albuquerque in 1993 by five Stanford University friends after M. Ries Robinson, MD, president of RGMT and a native New Mexican, returned home to obtain a medical degree from the University of New Mexico. Academic research in quantitative spectroscopy at the university led to partnering with Sandia National Laboratories. The collaborative effort led to a pursuit of commercialization ventures and the rest, as they say, has been a short and very successful history. The beauty of the high desert, combined with the cutting-edge research already being developed, made Albuquerque a natural choice for the new company's headquarters.

▶ RGMT lab techs inspect a blood sample to be used as a reference in a non-invasive measurement.

The research, development and design currently being done by RGMT are to support commercialization of non-invasive medical monitoring devices that will change the practice of medicine. Technical disciplines involved are project management, spectroscopy, optical, electrical, mechanical and software engineering. But RGMT believes in a work hard/play hard culture. The company's structure supports a matrix of cross-functional disciplines, and encourages every employee to challenge his or her technical expertise in a variety of topics. This grants each employee the opportunity to contribute to RGMT's bottom line as they contribute to their own growth as scientists and individuals, employees and family members. And RGMT is currently 100 percent employee owned.

An RGMT employee collects data from a test subject.

RGMT's values require a passion for excellence, the highest ethical standards in both work and professional conduct, teamwork and collaboration, clear and honest communication, professional and individual development, and fun.

And how are RGMT's mission and values reflected? In the company's reputation for outstanding research and development, and in its reputation as an outstanding place to work.

RGMT leads the way in research and quality of life, both on and off the job.

800 Bradbury Street SE, Suite 217, Albuquerque, NM 87106, 272-RGMT (7468), www.rgmt.com

283

the Spirit of
SUMITOMO SITIX SILICON, INC. est. 1994

Robert Montoya, an Advanced Material Processor, displays the next generation of wafer diameter: the 12-inch (300mm) epitaxial wafer.

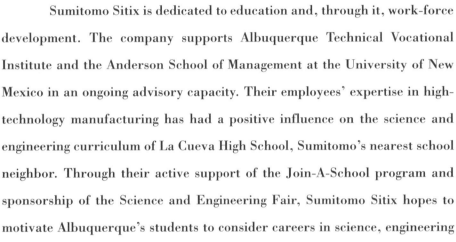

The most modern epitaxial manufacturing plant in the world makes its home in Albuquerque. Sumitomo Sitix Silicon, Inc., uses their proprietary technologies to produce superior quality silicon products for the semiconductor industry. Sumitomo Sitix is meeting future electronics demands for a variety of products, ranging from ultrapure silicon semi-conducting crystals to wafers of excellent grade and remarkable precision.

Sumitomo Sitix is dedicated to education and, through it, work-force development. The company supports Albuquerque Technical Vocational Institute and the Anderson School of Management at the University of New Mexico in an ongoing advisory capacity. Their employees' expertise in high-technology manufacturing has had a positive influence on the science and engineering curriculum of La Cueva High School, Sumitomo's nearest school neighbor. Through their active support of the Join-A-School program and sponsorship of the Science and Engineering Fair, Sumitomo Sitix hopes to motivate Albuquerque's students to consider careers in science, engineering

Standing over five feet tall, raw silicon ingots are sliced and polished to create the foundation for all integrated circuits.

and high-technology fields. The company employs 300 people in New Mexico, giving back a good job and a decent wage to local workers who make up 90 percent of their work force.

Ever mindful of their surroundings and the region's environmental concerns, Sumitomo Sitix and its neighbors on Balloon Fiesta Parkway recycle their water through Albuquerque's City Water Reuse Program, an idea that Sumitomo Sitix helped to develop with technical and financial support. The company has won a Green Zia award from the State of New Mexico's Department of the Environment for its conservation efforts. Sumitomo Sitix also has been recognized for their quality control programs with a Quality New Mexico Roadrunner Award.

Sumitomo Sitix is riding the wave of the future, intent on remaining the preeminent silicon epitaxial supplier in the world. They are equally committed to being a good neighbor within their Albuquerque community, a partner to education and a friend to the environment.

Sumitomo Sitix hopes to motivate Albuquerque students to consider careers in science.

9401 San Mateo Boulevard NE, Albuquerque, NM 87113, 346-6300, www.sitix.com

the **Spirit** of
VOICESTREAM WIRELESS est. 1995

VoiceStream Wireless has been helping New Mexicans GET MORE from their wireless phone service since 1996 and is committed to helping Albuquerque meet the opportunities of the 21st century. One of the fastest-growing wireless providers in the country, the company's growth paralleled and contributed to Albuquerque's growth throughout the latter half of the 1990s.

VoiceStream first began providing service in New Mexico in 1996 and subsequently opened Albuquerque's largest national customer care center in August of 1997. The 65,000-square-foot facility and 10,000-square-foot annex across the street combine to employ over 900 people. Additionally, VoiceStream sales and engineering staff employ over 100 people in the Albuquerque area. The company generates an estimated annual payroll of $10 million, and provides New Mexico and Albuquerque government entities with an estimated $12 million in tax revenues annually.

In 1999 VoiceStream announced plans to acquire Aerial Communications and Omnipoint, two wireless providers serving major markets in the Midwest and eastern U.S. Once completed, three out of every four Americans live in areas licensed to be served by VoiceStream or its affiliates, making the combined company one of the major providers of communications services in the country.

With its GET MORE promise to customers, nationwide expansion and dynamic spokeswoman, Jamie Lee Curtis, VoiceStream is building a strong, national brand in the wireless category, ensuring a long-term presence in the Southwest.

As VoiceStream expands service, Albuquerque citizens will continue to GET MORE FROM LIFE with technology-oriented careers, management opportunities and competitive salaries and benefits.

Actress Jamie Lee Curtis signed on as the company's spokesperson in 1998. Public appearances across the country included a surprise visit to the employees at VoiceStream's state-of-the-art Customer Care Center in Albuquerque (top right)

VoiceStream sells service in company-owned retail stores throughout Albuquerque/Santa Fe.

VoiceStream retail stores are located throughout the Albuquerque area. www.voicestream.com

the Spirit of
BANK OF ALBUQUERQUE est. 1998

▶

A teamwork approach and can-do attitude improve customer relations and make the Bank of Albuquerque a great place to work and bank.

With 15 branches and additional ATMs throughout the Albuquerque metro area, banking is at your convenience.

Through its vast array of products and its dedication to customer relationships, Bank of Albuquerque is providing New Mexicans a valuable alternative to the banking status quo. With 15 branches, the bank is specifically focused on New Mexico, and being part of a larger regional network allows it to offer the latest technology and financial services to its customers.

"We think Bank of Albuquerque offers a niche in the financial services community that is not really fulfilled by anyone else," says Greg Symons, President and CEO of Bank of Albuquerque. "We know from experience we have to provide a high level of personal service – that's the niche that has made our organization successful in our other markets. But we also realize that to do the best job for our customers we have to provide the latest product innovations and state-of-the-art technology. Because of our unique position, we have the ability to range across the large bank/small bank spectrum, providing both community bank service levels and a complete product line."

With its strengths and resources, Bank of Albuquerque is able to offer the entire range of consumer and commercial services and can meet the lending needs of the vast majority of the New Mexico community. Its locations offer quick turnaround and friendly service without the hassle of dealing with the slow, impersonal nature of many larger lending institutions. And with its 24-hour ExpressBank telephone bankers and website (www.bankofalbuquerque.com), its customers' personal needs can be met outside of traditional banking hours.

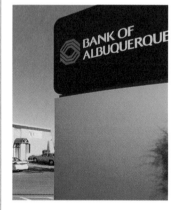

The bank is also dedicated to helping many charitable organizations in the state. "Banks have a symbiotic relationship with any community they operate in," Symons says. "The stronger the community's health and vitality, the healthier the banking system and vice versa – the stronger the banking system the more support we can provide back to the community. We're committed to making New Mexico and the communities we serve the best they can be."

"We're committed to making the communities we serve the best they can be."

PO Box 26148, Albuquerque, NM 87125-6148, 855-0855, www.bankofalbuquerque.com

In its relatively short history, Prinova Capital Group has emerged in Albuquerque as an important member of the financial services community. Prinova Capital Group consists of four primary entities: Factor Plus, Ltd., Prinova Investments, Ltd., Prinova Financial Consultants, Ltd. and Settlement & Recovery Company, Ltd. As a specialist in nontraditional forms of funding and finance, Prinova and its subsidiaries provide a single source of diversified services to a select group of businesses and individuals who may not meet traditional financing requirements or who may require highly specialized, skilled and experienced negotiation and facilitation services.

Regulated and insured financial institutions such as commercial banks are required to adhere to very strict guidelines. "Thank God for that," says Garcia emphatically. "If they are holding our money, it better be safe or they will lose the public's trust…and our money. Unfortunately, the rigidity of those institutions does not lend itself to the needs of growth companies and entrepreneurial endeavors." Prinova

"Today's business often demands viable alternatives to traditional financing sources," says President Vincent J. Garcia.

helps fill the void with a wide spectrum of financial products, such as:

• Purchase Order/Contract Financing • Factoring of Accounts Receivable • Letters of Financial Commitment • Credit Guarantees and Enhancements • Purchase of Nonperforming Debt • Preparation of Credit Proposals • Reciprocal Trade Exchanges • Real Estate Development.

A successful relationship with Prinova can elevate a company's financial performance to a level at which it can become qualified for traditional bank financing. For example, a company can start its relationship with Prinova by financing its purchase orders, graduating to factoring its accounts receivable, then securing a bank line of credit against accounts receivable with the assistance of Prinova. "Our goal is to help companies grow and make them healthy by utilizing their internal nonperforming assets. It is an absolute joy to see a company succeed because of our funding and other assistance we provide."

"It is an absolute joy to see a company succeed because of assistance we provide."

AFC-5, 2400 Louisiana Boulevard NE, Suite 260, Albuquerque, NM 87110, 881-0808, www.factorplus.com

▶

A new state-of-the-art call center was recently completed at Comcast Cable allowing for expanded customer service hours.

Comcast, formerly Jones Intercable, has been working hard to make Albuquerque a cable television and Internet mecca. By building improvements to its already top-notch infrastructure, including a new state-of-the-art 870 MHz platform, the company is going to put Albuquerque on the map as host to one of the fastest, most powerful and highest quality cable systems in the country.

The new platform will allow Comcast Cable to improve picture quality, enhance system reliability and add more channels. It will also allow the company to enter into the data services market, providing Internet connections and down the road, telephony to a market screaming for greater bandwidth.

Comcast Cable – and Jones before it – has also made a number of customer service improvements. Since Jones came to Albuquerque in 1986, the company has installed a state-of-the-art call center, expanded its telephone and office hours, added a number of payment options and implemented an on-time appointment guarantee. And Comcast, which bought Jones in 1999, continues to build on Jones' strong relationship with its customers.

Comcast Cable has begun a complete system upgrade which will bring digital service, and high-speed cable modem Internet access, to the Albuquerque area.

Comcast Cable and its employees also have a deep commitment to the Albuquerque community. From 1994 to 1999, Jones donated over $2.5 million worth of airtime to non-profit community organizations such as Pennies for the Homeless, Junior Achievement and the Make-A-Wish Foundation. It also has wired over 115 schools in the Albuquerque area with free cable and is in the process of connecting them with high speed cable modems at no charge. Comcast Cable further runs many scholarship and educational outreach programs, and its employees also have strong roots here, dedicating their energy to many local causes.

"I am especially proud of our employees who volunteer their time above and beyond their work to help make Albuquerque a better place for all of us. It is this sense of community that I continuously instill in my staff from the top down; it has become a basic premise of who we are," says Scott Binder, the company's Vice President and General Manager.

Comcast's employees have strong roots here, dedicating their energy to many local causes.

4611 Montbel Place NE, Albuquerque NM 87107, 344-0690, www.comcast.com

photography index

photography index
by page number

....

The Sandia Mountains border Albuquerque on the east. From the foothills to the 10,678-foot Sandia Crest, one passes through four of the earth's seven environmental zones. And on a clear day, the view from the Crest is more than 100 miles in all directions. The Sandia Peak Tram— the world's longest jigback tramway—will take you 2.7 miles to the 10,378-foot Sandia Peak for fine dining, skiing, hiking, biking and one of the most amazing views—and sunsets— you'll ever experience.

....

Route 66, the Mother Road—now Central Avenue —brought motels, neon and

newcomers to Albuquerque. The evolution of Route 66 reflects the growth of the entire city, and many of the architectural and design elements of yesteryear still live along Central as it cuts through the heart of the city

Albuquerque International Sunport uniquely combines the small-town southwestern charm of its past with a convenient and comfortable modernity. Beyond the nine major airlines and 147 daily flights that serve the Sunport, it also boasts a beautiful collection of public art and numerous concessions, shops and services.

For many, the old Alvarado Hotel was Albuquerque's center. It was port of entry and exit, meeting place, dining room and a great place to party or relax. Torn down in 1970, it is— at print time—being rebuilt and will again beat at the heart of Albuquerque. At the center of the city's

Downtown Revitalization, the Alvarado Transportation Center will be surrounded by new housing, entertainment, business and office complexes.

. . . .

. . . .

Local architecture reflects the area's past and future, as Pueblo revival meets Spanish revival and moves through the influences of every homebuilder, architect and developer who ever anchored in Bernalillo County.

. . . .

. . . .

The University of New Mexico is the region's educational and cultural center. UNM opened its doors in June of 1892 with an enrollment of 25 students. Today, with over 30,000 students, it's the state's largest university. From its trendsetting campus architecture by John Gaw Meem to its nationally ranked medical primary care curriculum, sports teams and theatrical presentations—UNM is a source of pride for all New Mexicans.

. . . .

. . . .

The neighborhoods of Albuquerque and the towns of Bernalillo County are as diverse and distinct as the people and cultures that populate this area. From the old adobe homes of the

North Valley to the high-end homes of Sandia Heights, from the rural sprawls of the South Valley to the planned communities of the Northeast Heights, the city grows and evolves, maintaining a balance of old and new.

110–111 large. Downtown Albuquerque, view from northeast. Jerry Rabinowitz

110 inset. Historic Albuquerque postcard, circa 1939. Courtesy of Foster Hurley

112–113 large. View from Albuquerque's High Desert. Jerry Rabinowitz

112 top. High Desert neighborhood home. Jerry Rabinowitz

113 top. Historic Albuquerque postcard, circa 1939. Courtesy of Foster Hurley

114–115 large. Sanitary Bakery, 907 South 2nd Street, 1918. 1975.063.753 gift of the Chiordi Family. Courtesy of Albuquerque Museum

115 inset. Fred's Bread and Bagels in Nob Hill. Wendy Walsh

116 Albuquerque aerial photograph. Marc Piscotty

117 Albuquerque aerial photograph. Marc Piscotty

118 Community Center volunteers. Michael Barley

119 Participant in crafts activity, Senior Day Care. Michael Barley

120 South Valley Boy Scouts. Michael Barley

121 Volunteer at Salvation Army Food Distribution center. Michael Barley

122 High school band member, Christmas Parade. Wendy Walsh

123 top left. Highland Community Center. Wendy Walsh

123 middle right. Sandia Casino dealer. Miguel Gandert

123 bottom. Wellness Center at Sandia Pueblo. Miguel Gandert

124 San Ignacio Church, Martineztown neighborhood. William Stone

125 Luminarias in Old Town on Christmas Eve. William Stone

126 Luminarias decorating the plaza in Old Town on Christmas Eve. William Stone

127 St. John's Episcopal Cathedral. Michael Barley

128 St. Joseph Square, St Joseph's Hospital. Robert Reck

129 top row from left. Altar piece on south Broadway; tattoo of Virgin Mary; house in Atrisco neighborhood; Henry Alderete and his lowrider. Miguel Gandert

129 bottom row, first two from left. 38 Trailer NW, Albuquerque; Stop the Violence campaign, downtown. Miguel Gandert

129 bottom row, third from left. Pimentel guitars. Jerry Rabinowitz

129 bottom row, fourth from left. Virgin Mary on south Broadway. Miguel Gandert

130 Street signs in High Desert. Robert Reck

131 Martineztown cemetery. Miguel Gandert

132 San Ignacio Statuary in Martineztown neighborhood. William Stone

133 top. Softball game in Martineztown neighborhood. William Stone

133 bottom. Martineztown neighborhood— Adobe home/San Ignacio church at dusk. William Stone

134 School on Wheels in Albuquerque's South Valley. Darren Poore

135 top left. Barelas bus stop. Darren Poore

135 right. Monument to Joseph Barelas. Darren Poore

135 bottom row. Tile mosaics, Barelas Park. Darren Poore

The Middle Rio Grande Valley has been occupied by Pueblo Indians since A.D. 500. By the 15th century it was home to roughly 15,0000 people who cultivated the land up and down the Rio Grande. These were the agricultural settlements that the Spanish found when they arrived in 1540, and it is this agricultural foundation that still thrives throughout Bernalillo County. Look for fields of green and livestock in towns, ranches and farms skirting Albuquerque and even within the city itself, in the South and North Valleys.

136 large. Red chile peppers hanging in ristras. Michael Barley

136 all insets. Sichler Farm in south Albuquerque. Wendy Walsh

138 top left. Clock tower, Los Ranchos de Albuquerque. Darren Poore

138 top right. Driveway off of North Rio Grande Boulevard. Darren Poore

138 bottom. Los Ranchos de Albuquerque Fire Department. Darren Poore

139 Vineyard and mountains–Anderson Valley Vineyard in the North Valley. Michael Barlev

140 South Broadway Cultural Center. Robert Reck

141 top. South Broadway Cultural Center. Robert Reck

141 bottom. South Broadway Cultural Center. Robert Reck

142 top left. Horses in the East Mountains. Darren Poore

142 top right. Triangle Grocery, East Mountains. Darren Poore

142 middle right. Tinkertown Museum, Sandia Park. Darren Poore

142 bottom left. Tinkertown Museum, Sandia Park. Jerry Rabinowitz

142 bottom right. Tijeras Library. Darren Poore

143 Corrales church. Jerry Rabinowitz

144 top left. Guadalupe Soza, Native American. Eric O'Connell

144 top right. Reuben Murray, executive director for Music Theater Southwest. Eric O'Connell

144 bottom left. Kevin Hagen, executive director of New Mexico Symphony Orchestra. Eric O'Connell

144 bottom right. Tom Jaeger, seven-time Olympic medalist in swimming. Eric O'Connell

145 top left. Ralph Berkowitz, classical pianist. Eric O'Connell

145 top right. Joe Powell, University of New Mexico Forensics. Eric O'Connell

145 bottom left. Lisa DiCarlo, music librarian for New Mexico Symphony Orchestra and amateur violinist. Eric O'Connell

145 bottom right. Paul Ford, University of New Mexico Theater professor. Eric O'Connell

146 top left. Angie Torres, actress. Eric O'Connell

146 top right. Troy Borron, architect and artist. Eric O'Connell

146 bottom left. Joel Gelpy, musical director for Music Theater Southwest. Eric O'Connell

The arts of Albuquerque and the cultures of the Southwest are intertwined. One is ever the reflection of the other, and it is all an integral part of life in Bernalillo County.

The New Mexico State Fair and the Kodak™ International Balloon Fiesta are two of the city's most popular events, but there's plenty more to see and do throughout the county: The Albuquerque Biological Park including the Botanic Gardens, the Aquarium, and the Rio Grande Zoo; the museums and galleries, sports events at every level; fiestas and festivals are a daily part of life in Albuquerque.

Albuquerque is surrounded by nature. Wilderness areas and open spaces are accessible from the Sandia Mountains in the east to the five dormant cinder cones and seventeen-mile long lava escarpment to the west. The Rio Grande and its bosque have been an oasis running through the center of the state for centuries. The city of Albuquerque has one of the most ambitious open space programs in the country— the city owns over 15,000 acres of open space land, and leases or jointly manages another 7,000 acres. The spaces are used for conservation, education, and—to the joy of all who live here or visit— recreation.

glosario

In the spirit of communication, in the spirit of respect, and in the spirit of New Mexico, we present a brief glossary of the Spanish words used in this book and in conversations throughout our city:

adobe	sun-dried clay brick
el camino	the road
corazón	heart
hacienda	ranch house
historia	history
mesas	plateaus
montañas	mountains
olla	stewpot
orgullo	pride
patrónes	bosses
portales	entrances, porches
ranchos	ranches
recuerdos	memories
saludos amigos	greetings friends
sin fronteras	without borders
tradiciónes	traditions
vida	life

glossary